COMPUTERS IN EDUCATION: LEGAL LIABILITIES AND ETHICAL ISSUES CONCERNING THEIR USE AND MISUSE

This monograph is a part of
The Higher Education Administration Series
which also includes:

☐ Administering College and University Housing:
   A Legal Perspective
☐ The Dismissal of Students with Mental Disorders:
   Legal Issues, Policy Considerations, and
   Alternative Responses
☐ A Practical Guide to Legal Issues Affecting College Teachers

Other Computer-Related Publications by the Author

Hollander, P.A., Young, D.P. and Gehring, D.D. (Eds.) (1983-)
    The Computer Law Monitor. Quarterly newsletter briefing
    of computer-related higher court decisions, plus checklists
    on relevant topics. Asheville, N.C. 28815-0267 (P.O. Box
    9267): Research Publications, Inc.

Hollander, P.A. (1984) An introduction to legal and ethical
    issues relating to computers in higher education. *Journal of
    College and University Law*, Fall, 11, 2, 215-232.

Hollander, P.A. (1983) University computing facilities: Some
    ethical dilemmas. In Baca, M.C. and Stein, R.H. (Eds.),
    *Ethical Principles, Problems, and Practices in Higher
    Education.* Springfield, Ill.: C.C. Thomas, Publishers.

COMPUTERS IN EDUCATION: LEGAL LIABILITIES AND ETHICAL ISSUES CONCERNING THEIR USE AND MISUSE

By Patricia A. Hollander, Esq.

The Higher Education Administration Series
Edited by Donald D. Gehring and D. Parker Young

COLLEGE ADMINISTRATION PUBLICATIONS, INC.

College Administration Publications, Inc.,
P. O. Box 8492, Asheville, N. C. 28814

Library of Congress Cataloging in Publication Data

Hollander, Patricia A.
    Computers in education.

    (The higher education administration series)
    Includes bibliographical references.
    1. Education law and legislation—United States.
2. Computers—Law and legislation—United States.
3. Liability (Law)—United States. 4. Education—
United States—Data processing. I. Title. II. Series.
KF4124.5.H65 1986   370'.28'54   86-2610
ISBN 0-912557-03-6

This publication is designed to provide accurate and authoritative information in regard to the subject matter covered. It is sold with the
understanding that the publisher is not engaged in rendering legal, accounting or other professional service. If legal advice or other expert
assistance is required, the services of a competent professional person
should be sought.

*—from a Declaration of Principles jointly adopted by a committee of the
American Bar Association and a committee of publishers.*

Table of Contents

Foreword

The use of computers in educational institutions is expanding at a rapid rate. As was true of slide rules in the past, many colleges and universities now require all incoming students to have a microcomputer. Even elementary and secondary schools are introducing computer literacy programs. Both of these factors demand that school administrators and faculties become aware of the legal and ethical parameters regarding computers.

The law in this field has not caught up with the technical advances. This monograph is designed to bring educators up to date with current legal and ethical issues relating to the computer. These issues involve every aspect of computer acquisition and use.

Knowledge in this area is absolutely imperative for educators, not only to protect themselves from legal liabilities, but also to protect their interest in computer programs and other software which they might create.

For those new to this field, this monograph includes an excellent glossary containing both legal and computer terminology. Checklists are also provided for those charged with making administrative decisions.

DDG
DPY
March, 1986

About the Author

PATRICIA A. HOLLANDER is an attorney in Buffalo, New York. Since 1972 she has been the General Counsel of the American Association of University Administrators, and has consulted extensively in the fields of education and computer law. She also speaks before many educational, computer and legal groups.

Ms. Hollander received her J.D. law degree from St. Louis University and did graduate work at Harvard Law School. At the State University of New York at Buffalo, she served for almost a decade as both an administrator and a faculty member in the School of Management and in the School of Law. In spring 1980, she taught at the University of Virginia's Center for the Study of Higher Education, as Visiting Professor.

Ms. Hollander is the author of *Legal Handbook for Educators*, published in 1978. She is co-author with John Pine of *The Public Administrator and the Courts*, published in 1985. She is also co-author of *A Practical Guide to Legal Issues Affecting College Teachers*, with D. Parker Young and Donald D. Gehring, published in 1985. Since its inception in 1983, she has been an editor of *The Computer Law Monitor*, a quarterly publication that summarizes in lay language significant court cases concerning computer technology.

Among her recent writings is the chapter, "University Computing Facilities: Some Ethical Dilemmas," she contributed to Baca and Stein's 1983 book, *Ethical Principles, Problems, and Practices in Higher Education*. Her article, "An Introduction to Legal and Ethical Issues Relating to Computers in Higher Education," appeared in the fall 1984 issue of the *Journal of College and University Law*. Also in 1984, her chapter, "The Chief Student Affairs Officer as Employer and Manager: A Special Risk," appeared in Owens' June 1984 book, *Risk Management and The Student Affairs Professional*, in the NASPA Monograph Series.

Chapter I

Roles of Law and Ethics Regarding Computers in Education

INCREASING USE OF COMPUTERS IN ADMINISTRATION, TEACHING AND RESEARCH

Educators at schools and colleges today—whether they serve as administrators, faculty, or staff—are faced regularly with new legal liabilities and ethical issues that arise out of the presence of computers in classrooms, offices, libraries, and labs. All levels of education—primary, secondary, and post-secondary—are affected. All educational tasks—administrative, teaching, and research—are involved.

The time is ripe, or overripe, for those with any degree of responsibility for computer-related activities at educational institutions to "learn the ropes and draw the lines."

Two Tasks for Educators

Educators will find they have two principal tasks concerning computer software and hardware.

One task is to manage the acquisition of computer software and hardware.

The other task is to manage the general use of computers once they are installed and, in particular, pay attention to the creation of new software and hardware by employees and students. For just as soon as people begin to become familiar with computers, they see ways of writing new programs and documentation, compiling new databases, or developing new hardware.

Every school and college needs policies to deal with the legal and ethical issues related to computers at their institution.

Emergence of "Computer Law"

The law of computers is, for the most part, the law of copyrights, patents, trademarks, and trade secrets. Computers fall into a category of property called intellectual property.

1

Software, that is, computer programs, documentation, and databases, generally is governed by copyright law.

Hardware, the computer machinery itself, such as keyboards, disk drives and video display terminals, usually is governed by patent law.

When information about new computer software or hardware is kept confidential, that information may be protected as a trade secret.

A logo or "mark" identifying a product or service may be protected as a trade mark or service mark.

Of course, there still will be many legal questions to be handled by the more well-established law of contracts or torts or criminal law.

Implications of New "Computer Law" for Academic Traditions

Traditionally in the academic community, copyrights usually were deemed to belong to the writers of the work, while patents generally were shared in some fashion between the inventor or discoverer and the educational institution.

Today, courts are being asked to apply copyright law and patent law to computer-related matters, and there are new interpretations evolving.

In addition, the many unusual features of computers also are having an impact on contract law, tort law, and criminal law. Even tax law requires rethinking in the light of new interpretations of tangible and intangible property.

TYPICAL LEGAL LIABILITIES AND ETHICAL ISSUES REGARDING COMPUTERS

Typical Legal Liabilities

On almost any ordinary day, educators at colleges and schools may be confronted with an array of legal questions concerning computers. They may arrive in the morning to find that the institution's chief executive office is ready to file suit because:

- the new computer acquired to handle graphics in color will do only word processing in black and white;
- the library's computerized circulation data has been destroyed;
- students have cracked an access code and gotten into the payroll files;
- a faculty member is about to file suit, claiming the copyright to the computer program she developed belongs to her personally, not to the institution; or
- a staff member is using unauthorized time on an institutional computer in the evening to conduct his real estate business.

If the right legal steps were taken in advance, the harried educator could respond that:

- the contract with the supplier of the new computer contains a warranty of fitness for a particular purpose so we will demand that the correct computer be supplied;

2

- we have back-up copies of the library circulation data secured in the safe in the business office;
- we will discipline the student in accordance with our written policy, change the access code more often, and consider setting up two separate, unlinked computer systems for student/classroom use and business use;
- our written policy regarding software created by faculty covers that situation, and in this instance the new program belongs to the faculty member; and
- our written policy regarding employee use of institutional computers for personal business covers that situation, and in this case had the employee requested permission, it would not have been granted, so a reprimand will be issued and placed in his personnel file.

Typical Legal/Ethical Issues

A typical legal/ethical issue might concern a student who cracked the access code; he ranks first in his class, says it was all in fun just to see if he was good enough to do it, did no damage other than breaking the code, and never before has been in trouble. Shall he be prosecuted criminally in addition to being disciplined by the institution?

The institution may have a policy allowing discretion in some instances of forgiving a first, minor transgression before moving to criminal prosecution.

Three Categories of Legal and Ethical Issues

The acquisition and use of computers by educational institutions generate at least three categories of legal and ethical issues.

The first category concerns relatively unique legal intellectual property issues, related to the law of copyrights, patents, trademarks, and trade secrets. Examples are: who owns the copyright on computer programs developed by faculty, staff, or students; and, may one make copies of computer programs? Computer hardware generally raises questions of patent law.

A second category relates to more common legal issues, such as contract issues regarding warranties covering computers, and tort issues regarding the negligent or wrongful use of computers. Criminal laws affecting computers fall into this category as well.

A third category arises from the fact that educational institutions often wish to respond to what may be termed legal/ethical issues in a different fashion than would noneducational organizations. For instance, educational institutions must decide whether every student who "breaks the code" of a computer to gain access to unauthorized time, for whatever reason, should be turned in for possible criminal prosecution as well as suffering campus penalties.

3

Institutional Liability Compared To Individual Liability

From the standpoint of the institution itself, civil liability may result in penalties such as injunctions and damages.

From the viewpoint of individuals, there may be both civil and criminal liabilities, possibly resulting in penalties including injunctions, damages, fines, and imprisonment. In addition, individuals may be subject to campus discipline, such as suspension, termination, or expulsion.

MAJOR AREAS OF LEGAL RISKS

Educators at schools and colleges will find risks of liability present in areas of computer-related activity such as:
- the process of acquiring computers, including deciding which computer or system to acquire, and negotiating acquisition contracts;
- the use of computer hardware and software at the institution, including setting policy for appropriate use and penalties for misuse of software and hardware, such as making unauthorized copies of computer software;
- faculty, administrator, and staff (employee) concerns, including making policy and rules regarding the ownership of copyrightable and patentable computer products created by employees;
- student matters, including making policy regarding the ownership of copyrightable and patentable products created by students;
- commercial exploitation of copyrighted and patented computer products developed by employees and students;
- negligence, including trying to avoid improperly programmed computers;
- security, including the protection of computer buildings, equipment, data, and files, and related concerns of privacy and confidentiality; and
- crime, including knowing what constitutes criminal activity and what the penalties are.

MAJOR LEGAL/ETHICAL ISSUES

A number of legal/ethical issues have been generated by the presence of computers at schools and colleges. Among them are:
- abuse of students, as where a faculty person, untrained in the use of computers, threatens a computer wise student that he will fail her unless she gets unauthorized computer time for him to do his research;
- abuse of computers by students, as in breaking an access code;
- responsibility to protect data, records, and research stored in computers;

4

- access to computers, as in providing opportunity for training in computer literacy;
- close questions regarding ownership of software created at the institution;
- competition for favor between computer-heavy and computer-light departments and individuals; and
- unknown physical dangers, such as radiation from video display terminals.

PRACTICAL GUIDE

This book is meant to be a practical guide that highlights basic legal and ethical questions and suggests specific preventive steps to help avoid some of the more obvious legal and ethical pitfalls related to the acquisition and use of computers in education. It gives tips on how to encourage appropriate use of computers and discourage misuse.

The book begins with some cautionary words about legal liabilities concerning the acquisition of computers.

Then, it moves on to legal issues related to the use and possible misuse of those computers in educational institutions. It also discusses a number of legal-ethical issues related to computers that are bound to arise in any educational enterprise.

RECOMMENDATIONS

Responsible educators at schools and colleges will want to take all reasonable measures to try to avoid computer-related risks. For instance:
- Institutional policy and related documents should reflect computer-related issues;
- Orientation and training of personnel and students on computer-related matters is essential;
- Maintenance of computer equipment must be top quality and ongoing; and
- Risk management, including security measures and insurance coverage, regularly must be reviewed and updated.

For further discussion, see:

Hollander, P.A., Young, D.P. and Gehring, D.D. (Eds.) (1983-) *The Computer Law Monitor.* Quarterly newsletter of briefs of court cases, plus checklists on relevant topics. Asheville, N.C. 28815-0267 (P.O. Box 9267): Research Publications, Inc.

Hollander, P.A. (1984) An introduction to legal and ethical issues relating to computers in higher education. *Journal of College and University Law,* Fall, 11, 2, 215-232.

Chapter II

Liability Related to the Acquisition of Computers

PRE-ACQUISITION PLANNING

Few acquisitions cry out for careful planning to the extent that computer acquisitions do. Choosing one computer or system over another sets patterns for carrying out the institution's tasks and commits substantial sums of money. It can have an affect on the entire institution, from its recruitment development, to curriculum development, to alumni development.

Educators at schools and colleges contemplating the acquisition of a single computer or several complex systems are confronted with the number one question: What do you want the computer to do for you? This is the first and most critical question to be answered. What functions are to be performed by the computer? Is the computer to drill students in math? Is it to collect data and create a database? Is it to provide word processing? Is it to be used in a research lab? Is it to produce payrolls? Will it be used by one person or by many?

From a legal standpoint, one reason this question is so crucial is that it is directly related to the degree of protection available from warranties. For instance, when you are able to set forth in an acquisition contract what functions a computer is to perform, a special kind of warranty may be created. It is called a warranty of fitness for a particular purpose. It says, in effect, that the computer supplier understands what special functions you expect the computer equipment to perform, that you are relying on his or her judgment to recommend appropriate equipment, and that the equipment being supplied will perform those functions. Then, should the computer fail to perform the expected functions—drilling students in mathematics, doing statistical research, handling student registration, or making out staff payroll checks—legal liability generally would rest with the computer supplier. The supplier would be responsible for repairing the computer, replacing the computer, paying damages, or doing a combination of these things.

On the other hand, where an acquisition contract merely states that a specified set of equipment is being ordered, without indicating what functions are to be performed, only the more ordinary warranty of merchantability may be created. A warranty of merchantability merely provides that the equipment will work properly, not that the equipment will perform particular functions such as those just mentioned above.

Ideally, both kinds of warranty ought to be sought. The warranty of merchantability will guarantee that the equipment will work properly. The warranty of fitness for a particular purpose will guarantee that the equipment supplied is the right equipment to perform the particular, expected functions.

Who Can Help Answer the Number One Question?

Get expert help in answering this question. This may be one of those rare occasions when a team or committee approach to solving a problem is both a real necessity and benefit.

Look for several kinds of experts. One set of experts will already be on the payroll or attending the school or college. They are the faculty, staff and students, in other words, the potential users of the computer. If the computer is to assist with teaching, then faculty and students may help define exactly how the computer is to be used in teaching. The computer may be expected to drill students by asking questions and providing correct answers. It may be expected to assist with grammar and composition. If, rather, it is to be used for payroll, then business office staff ought to be consulted.

A second set of experts needed consists of people knowledgeable about computers. You may have some of these people in-house. But, outside experts from computer software and hardware companies may be needed as well. They will have to deal with questions such as the following. What computer programs are available to do the tasks you want done? What kinds of computer equipment will be needed to run the programs? Will one computer keyboard do? Do you need a screen? Do you need a printer, and if so, should it be a letter quality printer or a less expensive and faster dot matrix printer? Will additional electrical outlets or other changes in present electrical equipment be needed? Are any structural modifications to the buildings required?

A third set of experts are the business office and legal people. They can help decide whether equipment should be leased or purchased. They will help negotiate warranties to cover poor performance of equipment. They may write into the acquisition contracts certain provisions for maintenance and updating of the computer as well as training of personnel.

Finally, it is a good idea to get an independent outside expert to look over all plans before the final decision is made. Find someone who has no particular ax to grind but is competent to understand your needs and make suggestions to improve the entire package.

How Many Computers or Systems?

A fairly standard set of computer equipment for a person who is doing word processing or simple accounting probably would consist of a suitable computer program, a computer keyboard, two disk drives, a screen, and a printer. The word processing or accounting program, along with an operating system program, would be inserted into the two disk drives. The operating system program, to run the system, would go into disk drive number one. The so-called applications program, to do the specific task such as word processing or accounting, would go into disk drive number two. The screen would be used to view work in progress. The printer would produce a paper copy of the work.

Can one get by with less? Yes, if all one wants to do, for instance, is drill students on spelling or math. Then, possibly a printer is not needed. The response on the screen of the monitor may be all that is required. No paper copy, sometimes called hard copy, is needed. Or the keyboard may have one disk drive built in, so all that is needed is one extra disk drive for the applications programs.

On the other hand, if more than one person will be using a computer, several computers may be needed. There are a number of ways of doing this. One way is to have a large "host" computer mainframe or microcomputer with many terminals. Another is to have personal computers, completely separate from one another at each desk or in each office. The possible combinations are vast.

Separate Systems

For security reasons as well as for efficiency reasons, it may be better to have two or three completely separate computer systems. One system may do all business activities, such as accounting and word processing. Another system may do only teaching related activities. Another would handle only research activities. Separate access codes and encryption mechanisms would exist for each separate system.

By having separate computer systems, legal liability connected with security of the equipment itself and with the confidentiality of the information contained in the equipment may be limited.

SELECTING A COMPUTER

Show Me!

Before a contract is written to rent or purchase a computer, ask as many questions about the computer software and hardware as you and your team of experts can think of.

Ask to see similar software and hardware actually functioning, wherever possible. Talk to the users of that equipment. Find out what their computer does well, and what their problems are.

Write into your contract as much protection as possible against similar negative events.

For example, if a computer "goes down," how much time is to be allowed for repairs or replacement before penalties are assessed for unreasonable delays? Is there a "standby" computer available somewhere to handle your work while your computer is being repaired or replaced?

Compatibility (Or Beware of Gifts)

All parts of a computer must be compatible, that is, consistent with the requirements of the basic operating system. Otherwise, they will not work. Make clear who is responsible for ordering all parts, so that liability for damages resulting from the ordering of noncompatible parts is placed properly.

A computer software program that does what you want but will not run on your existing computer hardware is hardly a bargain!

Gifts of computer software and hardware from computer manufacturers, wholesalers, and retailers may be tempting at first glance. But, before accepting any gifts, consider carefully who will pay if the gift items are not compatible with your present system. In the case of gift offers of large numbers of computers, think again whether you want to tie up your entire system with one particular brand of computer. Remember this is a gift with a possible long term string attached to it.

Think twice about compatibility of software and hardware. Liability for mistakenly acquiring noncompatible parts can be very costly where the institution is responsible for the action. The costs include time lost and replacement parts.

General Rule—Pick Software First, Then Hardware

The art of creating and developing software is such that finding software to perform the specific tasks desired may be difficult. Do not despair. Keep looking. Then, when you have found what you want, begin looking for various brands of hardware that will run it.

Do not sign a contract for hardware until you have located the software you want. Think of software and hardware as one complete unit, not two separate units, for one will not perform without the other.

If all else fails, and you cannot locate the software you need, there are several possible alternatives to consider. First, existing software may be adapted, customized, or modified to suit your needs. Second, a completely new software program can be developed especially for you. Both of these possibilities require the expertise of experienced computer programmers. You may have such programmers. You may wish to hire a person or firm to do the modifications or development for you.

Whether existing programs are to be adapted or new programs developed, the contracts for these services must be carefully written so as to provide for your testing the modified or new programs before formally accepting them. A fair amount of debugging and preparation of accurate documentation may be required. Payment should be due only after the programs are found to be exactly what you ordered.

NEGOTIATING CONTRACT TERMS

Are you purchasing a single personal computer or an entire computer system capable of multiple and complex operations?

In any event, you will be negotiating a sales contract.

You may be spending a few hundred dollars, a few thousand dollars, or tens of thousands of dollars. You may be dealing with a small, local, retail computer store or a large, distant, wholesale computer dealer.

Whatever the circumstances, there are several general rules to follow:

1. Know what you want the computer to do.
2. Get independent advice as to several brands and kinds of computers to see.
3. Ask to see the computer in operation, doing what you want it to do. Talk to people who are using it.
4. Get all the terms and conditions of the sale in writing to the extent possible.

Typical Acquisition Contract Terms

The terms and conditions of the contract begin with writing into the sales contract what it is we expect the computer to do, whatever components have been recommended by the salesperson.

Next, the software and hardware components themselves must be specified, unit by unit.

Are all components compatible? Are the various peripheral components compatible with the basic computer equipment? Is the telephone equipment compatible with the rest of the equipment?

The contract, also, must set out answers to questions such as the following:

What are the computer's performance expectations regarding; uptime and downtime, the numbers of users it will accommodate, the speed at which it will operate, whether statistics can be generated, whether reports can be produced in chart, table, or graph form.

Must there be special preparation of the site where the computer is to be housed, such as extra electrical power, heavy duty flooring, raised flooring to house cables, etc. Is air conditioning needed to off-set the heat generated by the computer? What site preparation will be done by the seller, and what will be done by the buyer?

Are there dates set forth for delivery, installation, testing of equipment? Is partial payment geared to these benchmark dates? What, if any, are the penalties for delay?

Will the equipment be installed completely by the seller, or will special outside technicians be required for some of the installation work?

What about documentation? Will the seller provide complete and accurate descriptive and instructional materials? What happens if additional materials are needed?

Will the seller's personnel be available to answer questions and give instructions? If so, can they be reached day and night, in person and by telephone?

Who will actually operate the computer equipment? Will it be operated by the buyer's personnel, the seller's personnel, or both? Will the seller's personnel train the buyer's personnel? If so, for how long? Who will train other employees hired later?

What about warranties? Have certain express warranties been made part of the contract? Are there other implicit warranties? A seller tends to wish to disclaim warranties. A buyer generally seeks to secure a warranty of fitness for a particular purpose, so that if the particular purpose is not achieved, both actual and consequential damages can be secured from the seller.

Has the seller arranged for the physical security of the computer equipment, as well as for the security of the data stored in the computer? Are there encryption devices? How is access to the computer controlled? Are there access codes, or other security devices? Is care being taken to reduce fire hazards? Who will train users and other personnel about these matters?

Have arrangements been made for the making and storing of backup copies of computer programs? Storage should be in some other physical location, in a fireproof vault or deposit box. (Incidentally, diskettes require a greater degree of protection, regarding moisture and temperature, than normal "fireproof" safes provide.)

How will maintenance of equipment be provided? Will the seller provide maintenance? Will an outside firm do it? Will the buyer undertake maintenance? What exactly does the maintenance contract provide?

What about emergencies? Suppose the computer "crashes" or "goes down" right in the midst of student registration, or during a payroll run? Is there other equipment that the seller will make available to the buyer so that jobs can be completed without substantial loss of time or money?

Suppose in the future certain modifications need to be made in computer programs or equipment. How will these costs be handled by the seller? Are there discounts available?

Suppose your vendor goes bankrupt. What arrangements have been made to retain access to the updated source code, such as placing it in escrow and keeping it updated?

Financial matters to be settled include the following. Are terms clearly stated regarding rental, purchase, leasing, time-sharing and service-bureau arrangements? What discounts may be applicable now and regarding future dealings? What tax issues may impact the financial package? Are penalties set forth regarding both non or partial performance by the seller and non or partial payment by the buyer?

What insurance coverage should there be for damage to, or injury resulting from, the equipment or the personnel who use it? Is there insurance coverage of possible loss of business?

WARRANTIES

There are a number of warranties possible, such as express warranties that set forth exactly what is warranted, and implied warranties, such as an implied warranty of merchantability or an implied warranty of fitness for a particular purpose. Generally, the warranty that turns out to be of greatest help in a large number of cases is an implied warranty of fitness for a particular purpose.

Warranty of Fitness for a Particular Purpose

Suppose you told a software salesperson that you wanted a computer program that would help your students type class themes and papers, and that you were interested especially in a program that could deal with all those footnotes! You bought the program the salesperson recommended, but when you actually tried it, there was no way for the program to handle footnotes. Is there not some kind of a warranty on which you might rely to try to get your money back?

Yes, there is. The warranty is known as an implied warranty of fitness for a particular purpose. That is, it is a warranty that computer software or hardware is suitable for the special purpose of the buyer, which will not be satisfied by mere fitness for general purposes.

An implied warranty of fitness for a particular purpose arises in just such a situation as the one described above. There, a person set forth the specific functions a program was to do, and relied on the expert advice of the salesperson as to which program to select. By recommending a particular program as one that would meet the specific needs stated, the salesperson warranted that the program recommended was fit for the particular purpose set forth.

An implied warranty of fitness for a particular purpose provides much more legal protection than the more ordinary implied warranty of merchantability.

Warranty of Merchantability

An implied warranty of merchantability merely warrants that a computer is reasonably fit for the general purpose for which it was sold. It does not warrant that it will do anything in particular, such as handle footnotes, or operate at a specific speed, or accommodate manuscripts of a particular length. The seller will have met his responsibility if, for instance, a word processing program does word processing. Only if the word processing program fails to do general word processing, could a buyer claim that the implied warranty of merchantability was breached.

Implied Warranty Compared to Express Warranty

The two warranties just discussed are "implied" warranties. There also are "express" warranties.

An express warranty is one that a buyer and seller usually discuss in detail during negotiations for the acquisition of a program or hardware. An express warranty often is written. A seller expresses exactly what the program or equipment is expected to do. Where there is an express warranty, a buyer generally would have unquestioned recourse to legal redress if the program or other equipment fails to meet the terms of the express warranty.

REMEDIES FOR POOR PERFORMANCE

When a computer does not function properly, there are a number of possible remedies available, depending on the facts of each situation. Breach of contract, claims of misrepresentation and fraud, and violation of state deceptive trade practices acts are common legal theories utilized by purchasers of faulty computer equipment.

Breach of Contract

A breach of contract suit may allege that the seller did not provide the specific computer equipment set out in the sales contract. Or, the breach of contract claim could be that the equipment was not delivered on time, or that only part of the equipment was delivered, or that testing was not done, or the documentation was inadequate or that certain components were incompatible.

Money Damages

Two kinds of money damages may be available. One would be actual damages, and the other would be consequential damages.

For instance, a suit involving a breach of warranty regarding the proper functioning of a computer system resulted in actual damages amounting to the difference between the value of the computer system as delivered and the value of the system as warranted. The amount of damages awarded was over $200,000. *Chatlos Systems, Inc* v. *National Cash Register Corp.*[1]

Consequential damages could be, for example, the monies foregone by a buyer due to the loss of business that was foreseeable by a seller if the wrong computer were delivered.

Misrepresentation

In one case, a court found that a seller negligently misrepresented the capability, suitability, reliability, serviceability, and profitability of a computerized typesetting machine, known as the EditWriter 7500. Evidence produced at the trial showed that the EditWriter did not function as represented. "The RAM board was not functional; the keyboard locked up; the viewing screen blanked out or information shown on the screen did not transfer to the photo unit; the photo unit produced crooked lines, bouncy type, spontaneous capitalization, and shadow images. The disk drive alignment malfunctioned, erasing information recorded onto the floppy disks." The appeals court awarded damages of $117,797.55, including the value of data stored in the machine, lost profits, employees' wages, and the purchase price of the machine. *Barnard* v. *Compugraphic Corporation,*[2]

State Statutes—Deceptive or Unfair Trade Practices

The following situation is a classic illustration of a violation of a state statute prohibiting deceptive or unfair trade practices. Evidence showed that a seller intentionally made fraudulent representations about the state of development of its applications software products in order to induce a buyer to enter into a distributorship contract. The court found that the seller "willfully or knowingly" violated the Massachusetts unfair trade practices act. The award to the buyer was over $4 million. *Computer Systems Engineering, Inc.* v. *Quantel Corp.*[3]

RECOMMENDATIONS

Provide adequate time and support for pre-acquisition planning.

Decide what you want your computer to do.

Ask to see computers in operation like the one you want.

Talk to users of computers like the one you want about their experience.

Do your best to see that the written acquisition contract for your computer contains all the terms and conditions of concern to you.

---

[1]Chatlos Systems, Inc v. National Cash Register Corp. 670 F. 2d 1304, U.S. Court of Appeals for Third Circuit, 1982.

[2]Barnard v. Compugraphic Corporation, 667 P. 2d 117, Court of Appeals of the State of Washington, 1983.

[3]Computer Systems Engineering, Inc. v. Quantel Corp. 571 F. Supp. 1365 and 1379, U.S. District Court for the District of Massachusetts, 1983.

Pay special attention to contract provisions concerning testing of equipment, payment over time as testing benchmarks are passed, updating of equipment (especially software), maintenance, training of users, warranties, and provisions for standby equipment.

Chapter III

Liability Regarding Copying and Use of Computer Programs

Educators at schools and colleges will recognize the need for the development of policies and regulations for classroom and general use of the institution's computers.

In addition to the usual concerns, computers raise the unique legal problem of possible copyright infringement when copies are made of computer software programs. The relative ease and speed with which even novices can make copies of costly, copyrighted computer software programs causes serious exposure of the institution to potential claims of copyright infringement.

Schools and colleges sometimes sell computer equipment at discount to employees and students. This, too, may present legal problems.

MAKING COPIES OF SOFTWARE PROGRAMS

Inevitably, a question arises about the legality of making copies of computer programs. Here are a few of the most common situations.

Back-Up and Archival Copies

First of all, there is the question of whether backup or archival copies of a software program one has purchased outright are lawful. The answer is yes. When a software program is acquired through an outright purchase, the federal Copyright Act specifically provides that backup copies can be made for archival purposes.

The copyright law states:

. . . it is not an infringement for the owner of a copy of a computer program to make . . . another copy . . . of that computer program provided: . . . (2) that such new copy . . . is for archival purposes only and that all archival copies are destroyed in the event that continued possession of the computer program should cease to be rightful. 17 U.S.C. Sec. 117 (1980).

Copyright law would not apply, however, where one is not the owner of a program, but a licensee. One then would be bound by the terms of the license contract secured from the copyright owner.

"Shrink-Wrap" Licenses and the License vs. Sale Contract

Educators purchase many computer programs. Buyers of computer programs may say, "I thought when a person bought a copy of a software program, the person became the owner of that copy. Now I hear that sometimes the buyer becomes a licensee, not an owner. What in the world does that mean?

A license rather than a sale could occur where the software purchased was sealed closed in such a fashion that when a buyer tore open the seal, he or she found inside a paper saying the purchaser had been given a license by the copyright owner to use the copy of the program in certain limited, specified ways. This is known as a "tear open" or "shrink wrap" license. A buyer then would be a licensee, bound by the terms of the license from the copyright owner. Conceivably, a license may not permit backup copies.

There are legal questions still unanswered about whether a buyer, who thinks he is becoming the owner of a copy, instead becomes only a licensee, when, in fact, the buyer does not learn about the license until after he has paid for the program and opened the package.

Louisiana has passed legislation recognizing shrink-wrap licenses.

Avoiding the Sale vs. License Controversy

Is there anything one can do to avoid the controversy about whether a buyer who opens a "shrink-wrap" or "tear open" software program is an owner or a licensee of the copy of the program?

One way to avoid the license question would be to negotiate a true purchase agreement directly with the owner of the copyright. This is easier done if one is buying a large computer system, such that one is in direct communication with the owner of the copyright. It is not usually possible when one walks into a neighborhood computer shop and purchases a program there.

In general, legal experts believe that buyers of "shrink-wrapped" programs may assume they are owners of the program they purchased, on the following grounds. Such purchasers are unaware of the alleged license until after they buy the program and tear open the package. They could not be said to have known or agreed to the license arrangement. Therefore, the license is ineffective. As mentioned elsewhere, however, at least one state, Louisiana, has legislated a shrink-wrap license law, which has yet to be tested in the courts.

Copies for Friends and Co-Workers

Sometimes, the "May I copy?" scenario goes like this. "I bought a terrific word processing program, and now some of my friends and co-workers want me to make copies for them. May I make copies for them and charge them what the program cost me, or at least the cost of making a copy? If I may not charge for the copy, may I give it to them free?"

The answer is ABSOLUTELY NOT! Remember that the owner of the copyright of the program has placed the copyright on the program in order to protect it from use without appropriate permission or payment. The copyright owner wants the computer program used by many, many people. But, the copyright owner wants to be paid for that use. Or, at least be asked for permission to use the program. Each time you make an unauthorized copy, whether you sell that copy or give it away, you are depriving the copyright owner of payment for use of the program. You are infringing the copyright owner's exclusive right to earn money through the sale of the copyrighted program.

However, merely lending one's own copy to others does not appear to be an infringement.

Keep in mind that you might be a copyright owner someday!

Copying Your Office Program to Use at Home

The same negative answer goes for a query about whether one can make a copy of a computer program bought for use at the office in order to use it at home.

It is an infringement of copyright to make a copy of an office program for use at home. However, one could get permission from one's employer to borrow the office copy, take it home and use it there, then return it to the office.

Copy Bought for One Department Duplicated for Use by Another Department

A computer program bought by one department cannot be copied for use by another department. Where a single program will be useful to many departments, either buy enough copies for all departments, or consider negotiating a site license that will cover multiple copies at less cost.

ADAPTATIONS OF COMPUTER PROGRAMS

The Copyright Law permits the owner of a copy of a computer program to make an adaptation in order for the program to be used in conjunction with a particular set of computer equipment.

However, an adaptation may be transferred only with the authorization of the copyright owner. 17 U.S.C. Sec. 117.

An adaptation is not considered to be a new work. The individual who makes the adaptation is not considered to be the owner of it.

19

FAIR USE OF COMPUTER PROGRAMS

Computer programs are protected by copyright as a form of "literary work." Thus, in attempting to sort out questions of fair use of computer programs, it may be helpful to think of a computer program as though it were a book. Generally a copyrighted book cannot be copied without permission of the copyright owner. Similarly, a copyrighted computer program generally cannot be copied without the permission of the copyright owner.

Fair Use Defined

Fair use is a statutorily created (Sec. 107 of the 1976 Copyright Act), permissible use of copyrighted works under certain limited circumstances notwithstanding the rights of the copyright owner.

Fair use of a copyrighted work includes:

reproduction in copies . . . for purposes such as criticism, comment, news reporting, teaching (including multiple copies for classroom use), scholarship, or research . . ..

Fair use is not an infringement of copyright.

Four Factors Determine Fair Use

In determining whether a particular use of copyrighted work, such as a computer program or a book, is a fair use, consider:

1. the purpose and character of the use, including whether of a commercial or nonprofit educational purpose;
2. the nature of the copyrighted work;
3. the amount and substantiality of the portion used in relation to the copyrighted work as a whole; and
4. the effect of the use on the potential market for or value of the copyrighted work.

Regarding the first of the above factors, the purpose and character of the use, while the doctrine of fair use applies generally to educational settings, the mere fact that copies of a textbook or a computer program are made for a nonprofit educational purpose will not provide an automatic "fair use" defense against a charge of infringement. Textbooks and computer programs are meant for sale to the educational market. The way for an educational institution to get more copies is to buy them, not duplicate them. Bulk purchases of software or negotiation of a site license permitting use of a program throughout a designated site, such as a whole building, campus, or system, are other avenues to pursue.

As to the second factor, the nature of the copyrighted work, most computer programs may be likened to technical writings like operator's manuals. These usually are deemed to be informational rather than creative writings, so fair use could be available as a defense, other facts permitting.

Concerning the third factor, the amount and substantiality of the portion used, the tests applied here involve both quantity—how much was copied—and the importance to the work of that which was copied. As to quantity, excerpts usually are acceptable fair use. Congress contemplated "reproduction by a teacher or student of a small part of a work to illustrate a lesson."[1] Thus, in the case of books, an excerpt could illustrate grammar and the author's style. In the case of computer programs, an excerpt could illustrate programming techniques and show what is source code as compared to object code.

What Is NOT Fair Use

Few would say that copying a whole book for use by students was a fair use. Yet, some try to maintain that copying an entire computer program for use by students is a fair use. Both these copying practices clearly are copyright infringements in all but extraordinary circumstances.

Questions About Fair Use of Owned Copies

Q. May we purchase one copy of a computer program and use it to make twenty other copies for use by students?

A. No, Section 107 of the Copyright Act prohibits reproduction of computer programs in copies and distribution of copies to the public without permission.

Q. May we purchase one copy of a computer program and transfer it from floppy disk to hard disk for use with our hardware?

A. Yes, Section 117 of the 1980 amendments authorizes adaptation as an essential step in the utilization of the computer program with a machine.

Q. May we make a back-up copy of a purchased program?

A. Yes, Section 117 also authorizes a back-up copy.

Q. May we lend our copy of a purchased program to students in serial fashion?

A. Yes, just as you would lend a library copy of a book to students in serial fashion. However, it is not permissible to permit all students to have copies of the program simultaneously, just as it would not be permissible to make enough copies of a book so that all students could have copies simultaneously.

Q. If we purchase twenty copies of a program for use by students in one class, may we use the same twenty copies for a subsequent class?

A. Yes, you may own multiple copies of a computer program and lend them, just as you would lend textbooks. Also, remember to make back-up copies of any programs lent out in case they are destroyed.

---

[1]U.S. Congress, House Judiciary Committee, 90th Cong., 1st Sess., 1967, H.R. Rep. No. 90-83 ("1967 House Report") at 65.

Q. Suppose we are sued by a copyright owner who claims we are aiding and abetting students who make personal copies from the copies we lend them?

A. Reasonable precautions in the classroom to attempt to prevent unauthorized copying will be very helpful in countering such a charge.

Q. Is there some way we can acquire multiple copies of software other than buying them piecemeal?

A. Consider trying to negotiate bulk purchases or persuading software companies to donate copies under tax-favored conditions.

Fair Use of Copies Acquired by License

Where copies of software are not owned, but licensed from the owner, the terms of the license control what copies may be made.

Consider negotiating a site license that will cover use of the software throughout the designated site, such as an entire building, campus, or system. Consider also persuading licensors to donate permission to use.[1]

"PUBLIC DOMAIN" COMPUTER PROGRAMS

Computer programs created by individuals supported in their task by public funds, such as government research grants, often are owned by the government. They are said to be in the "public domain," and may be freely copied and used.

PENALTIES FOR COPYRIGHT INFRINGEMENT

Penalties for copyright infringement include the following:
1. Injunctions against further infringing use;
2. Impoundment and destruction of infringing articles;
3. Actual damages and profits attributable to the infringement;
4. Statutory damages;
5. Costs and attorney's fees; and
6. Criminal prosecution (fine and/or imprisonment and seizure of infringing articles).

—17 U.S.C. Secs. 502-509

Registration Necessary to Sue

Registration of a work with the Copyright Office is a prerequisite to filing suit for infringement of a copyright and seeking an award of damages or fees. —17 U.S.C. Sec. 412.

COPYING DEEMED PLAGIARISM

In addition to being unlawful as an infringement of copyright, copying a protected computer program may be deemed plagiarism, just as would copying any other intellectual work.

---

[1]For further discussion of fair use, see: Brooks, D.T. (1985) Fair use of computer software by educators. EDUCOM Bulletin, Summer 1985, Vol. 20, No. 2.

A school or college should state in its policies or rules what penalties are possible as a result of students' or faculty members' or staff members' copying all or part of a protected computer program and attempting to pass it off as their own work.

MAKING LAWFUL COPIES OF SOFTWARE PROGRAMS

Here is what most legal commentators presently believe one may do with the copy of a computer program one owns:

- "copy" it by using it in a computer's memory;
- make one backup or archival copy;
- make adaptations in order to use in a particular machine;
- lend it; and
- sell it; in which case the backup or archival copy must be destroyed.

Educational institutions also are permitted "fair use," such as copying brief excerpts to demonstrate a programming technique.

SALES AT DISCOUNT BY SCHOOLS OR COLLEGES

Computers sometimes are offered for sale at a discount to teachers, students and staff by schools or colleges that have negotiated discount arrangements with computer companies.

These discount sales may be fought by local computer merchants.

In one instance, a state university, the University of Illinois at Urbana-Champaign, closed its computer-discount store after suit was filed by four computer store owners who alleged the university was in violation of a state statute that prohibits it from interfering with private enterprise. The university turned over the discount sales to a local Computerland store.[1]

In another case, the Board of Regents of the University of Wisconsin System had an agreement with Apple to sell computers to students and staff. The prices charged by the university for resale to staff and students often were lower than those charged by Apple to it's local authorized dealer. The local Apple dealer sued both Apple and the university.

On one issue, the U.S. District Court of the Western District of Wisconsin found in favor of Apple in that Apple expressly had reserved to itself in the dealership contract the right to make unlimited resales and direct sales without notice or liability to the dealer.

On another issue, the court found in favor of the state university system by holding that the university system was entitled to Eleventh Amendment immunity from liability as an entity of the state.

However, on a third issue concerning a possible violation of the Robinson-Patman Price Discrimination Act, the court said it could

---

[1]Chronicle of Higher Education, March 8, 1985, p. 18, col. 2.

not grant Apple's request for a summary judgment because there remained material factual disputes about whether Apple's defense under the Nonprofit Institutions Act was sufficient. At issue was whether the provision that university resales to staff and students were conditional on no further resale by staff and students provided enough of a limitation on the discount program to permit the program to be deemed to have an educational purpose. These facts would have to be determined at a trial.[1]

RECOMMENDATIONS

Develop and disseminate a written policy regarding the making of copies of computer software.

Before selling computer products at discount to employees and students, have your legal counsel review the proposal.

---

[1]Computronics, Inc. v. Apple Computer, Inc. and the Board of Regents of the University of Wisconsin System, 600 F. Supp. 809, U.S. District Court for the Western District of Wisconsin, 1985.

Chapter IV

Liability Regarding Creation of New Computer Software or Hardware by Employees and Students

Schools and colleges will find it useful to have a stated policy with regard to legal protection and ownership of computer software and hardware created by employees, such as faculty, staff and administrators, and by students.

Early clarification of ownership is especially crucial concerning computer software. Whoever is determined to be the "author" of copyrightable works, e.g. computer programs, documentation, and databases, now has instantaneous automatic copyright protection in those works as soon as they are in fixed, tangible form. Therefore, even before work begins, the parties should know who is the legal author.

For example, regarding employees, is the employee or the employer the author? In the case of students, is the student or the institution the author?

At most educational institutions, the tradition is that copyrights belong to the writer, unless there is a contract or other agreement to the contrary.

As for computer hardware, patent law generally applies. The tradition at educational institutions usually is that patents are taken out in the name of the individual employee-inventors and then assigned to the institution. Revenues may be shared.

Whatever the arrangement is, regarding ownership of intellectual property, it should be fully understood by all parties, including students, and, preferably, should be in writing.

COMMERCIAL EXPLOITATION OF COMPUTER SOFTWARE AND HARDWARE CREATED BY EMPLOYEES AND STUDENTS

Schools and colleges should have a stated policy concerning possible commercial exploitation of computer products created by employees and students. Where support services for commercial exploitation are available, they should be described.

Where educational institutions choose to market software, for example, the financial return may be substantial. Stanford University expects to earn some $600,000 this year by licensing software written by Stanford faculty members, staff members and students. Stanford has had a software licensing service for commercial exploitation of Stanford-created software products since 1982. Engineering and computer science produce most of the software, ranging from a program that collects data for biology experiments to "Mozart," a program that projects attendance at musical performances.[1]

Pricing of Computer Products

Any school or college contemplating the marketing of software or hardware must make several threshold decisions; for instance, whether to have different pricing policies for software sold to commercial companies as compared to those sold to educational and governmental agencies. Stanford's policy requires commercial companies to pay from $500 to $10,000 to use the programs, while universities and government agencies pay only the distribution costs, which are said to be about $200 for programs for mini- and main-frame computers.

Stanford also has a number of licensing agreements that allow commercial publishers to market computer programs that the publishers have brought up to commercial standards through additional testing and by writing user manuals.

Revenue Sharing

A school or college also must have a policy regarding how revenue from products it markets will be shared. Stanford, for instance, treats income from software licenses it markets like income from patents: one-third goes to the author of the software, one-third to her school within the university, and one-third to her department.

Non-School Marketing

Stanford reports that not all Stanford-created programs are marketed through the university. Some software writers choose to go directly to commercial publishers and negotiate their own arrangements.

Ownership

To reiterate, each educational institution must clarify its policies concerning ownership of software created by its employees and students. Stanford's policy is that the copyright belongs to the writer unless the software is written under contract or agreement with the university.

[1]Chronicle of Higher Education April 10, 1985, p. 28, col. 1.

Confidentiality Agreements

In order to legally protect a new work or a trade secret not protected by copyright or patent, it is useful to ask persons with whom a new work or trade secret is to be discussed to sign a confidentiality agreement or trade secret status reminder letter. This would be appropriate, for example, in discussing a new work or a trade secret with a prospective financial backer.

A confidentiality agreement or trade secret status reminder letter states that the new work or trade secret, such as a computer program, code, documentation, data base or customer list, is considered confidential and/or a trade secret, and is not to be divulged or used by parties who have not received written permission from the owner.

LEGAL PROTECTION OF COMPUTER SOFTWARE BY COPYRIGHT

Most computer software programs are protected by copyright. Some are protected by trade secret. In rare situations, usually where a computer program is part of a larger process or machine, programs may be protected by patent.

In the early days of the development of computer programs, there was a legal question as to whether they were in fact copyrightable. There was never any real question about whether computer hardware was patentable.

The copyrightability of computer programs finally was settled in a case called *Apple Computer Inc.* v. *Franklin Computer Corp.*[1] The court held not only that computer programs were copyrightable, but went on to say that computer programs are copyrightable whether written in source code or object code, whether embodied in floppy disks or silicon chips, and whether they are applications programs or operating system programs.

TRANSLATIONS OF COMPUTER PROGRAMS FROM ONE COMPUTER LANGUAGE TO ANOTHER

Where a computer program written in one language, such as Event Driven Language (EDL), is translated to another computer language, such as BASIC, to run on different computer equipment, the translated program generally is not considered to be a new work. A translated program generally is deemed to be a derivative work. The owner of the copyright in the original work generally would be deemed to be the owner of the copyright in the derivative work.

Thus, the copyright covering a computer program written in one language may be infringed by a substantially similar program written in another language. Studying the source code of a copyrighted

---

[1]Apple Computer Inc. v. Franklin Computer Corp., 714 F. 2d 1240, U.S. Court of Appeals for the Third Circuit, 1983 (settled Jan. 4, 1984).

computer program and then substantially reproducing its manner of operation in another computer language may lead to charges of copyright infringement.[2]

DERIVATIVE WORKS

Customizations and enhancements of existing computer programs usually are deemed to be derivative works, not new works. Conversions, too, have been found to be derivative works.

Generally, a derivative work belongs to the owner of the original work.

Even where a modified computer program is two-thirds the work of a second party and appears to be "new," the modified work may belong to the owner of the original work.

There may be situations where a second party could find a way to separate his or her work from the original and claim ownership of that part.

In most instances, however, starting with a program owned by another, with no real break in the connection between the two, leads to a modified work owned by that other.

To use such a modified work, one should have the authorization of the original owner. One could pay for such authorization, get it gratis, or arrange a form of shared ownership.

One of the first cases to find that a conversion of a computer program was a derivative works is *SAS Institute, Inc.* v. *S & H Computer Systems, Inc.*[3] The facts in that case led the court to find that there was no real break in the connection between the original program and the modified program.

COPYRIGHT AND PATENT PROTECT EXPRESSION AND EXECUTION OF IDEA, NOT IDEA ITSELF

When a computer program, documentation, or data base is copyrighted, only the expression of the idea, not the idea itself, is protected.

Therefore, it is entirely possible that someone else may come up with another computer program, documentation, or data base expressing the same idea in a different form of expression, and copyright the new work.

For example, there are any number of copyrighted computer programs that do word processing. The idea of doing word processing

[2]Whelan Associates v. Jaslow Dental Laboratory, U.S. District Court for the Eastern District of Pennsylvania, 609 F. Supp. 1307, 1985, and 609 F. Supp. 1325, 1985.
[3]SAS Institute, Inc. v. S & H Computer Systems, Inc., 605 F. Supp. 816, U.S. District Court for the Middle District of Tennessee, 1985.

is not copyrightable. Particular computer programs embodying different ways to do word processing are copyrightable.

Similarly, a patent protects the form of execution of an idea, not the idea itself. The idea of inventing computer hardware to display information on a video screen may be executed in different ways, each of which may be patented.

Examples of Copyrightable Software

Here are some examples of computer software and ancillary material that could be protected by copyright:

Operating Systems Software Program—
A basic program that actually causes the computer to operate. It usually is written in "object code," that is, a computer language that is readable only by a machine, rather than in "source code," which is readable by humans;

Applications Systems Software Program—
A program designed to accomplish a particular task, such as, registration of students, payroll, or accounts receivable;

Database—
A compilation of information, such as a list of current faculty, staff, and students, or a bibliography of references to computer crime;

Flow Chart—
A written representation of the steps or logical components used in analyzing a problem, often used by programmers to set forth the sequence of commands in a program;

Listing
Computer-printed representation of a program, showing the input or output data resulting from a command to "print" or "list;"

Documentation—
A manual or other written document prepared for systems analysts and programmers explaining, for instance, how to operate a computer system or program. It usually also contains specifications.

Operations or Service Manual—
A written explanation of how a computer system or program operates, prepared for use by persons expected to operate the system or program or provide maintenance;

Updates—
Improvements made to program code, date, documentation, or manuals to correct errors or improve operation. May refer also to new versions of the software for use with new or different hardware. Sometimes called "patches."

RIGHTS OF COPYRIGHT OWNER

A school or college may be the copyright owner of a computer program. Or, the copyright owner may be a faculty member, a staff member, an administrator, or a student.

The owner of the copyright of a computer program or other work has five exclusive rights. The copyright owner may do, or authorize others to do, the following:

1. reproduce copies of the program or work;
2. prepare derivative works, that is, adapt or modify the program; (Note: A modified program may or may not be a new work. Generally, the original parts of the program belong to the owner of the original parts, and the new modifications belong to the author of the new parts. If the owner of the original parts is also the author of the modifications, there is no problem. But, if the original parts are owned by one person, and a different person is the author of the modifications, ownership of the total modified program needs to be clarified.)
3. distribute copies of the program by sale or other transfer of ownership, or by rental, lease, or lending;
4. perform the program or work, that is, play video games in arcades;
5. display the program or work; that is, exhibit the program or listings at conventions and other meetings.

Joint Owners of a Copyright

Who owns the copyright if there are more than one author?

If there are joint authors, they are co-owners, that is tenants in common.

Each joint owner has the right to use or license the computer program, and then must account to the other joint owners.

REGISTRATION OF A COPYRIGHT

Why Officially Register a Computer Program?

A client may ask an attorney, "If it is true that under the new Copyright Act, computer programs are protected by copyright from the moment of creation, why should I go to the trouble of getting a Certificate of Registration from the U.S. Copyright Office?"

The answer is that you will need the Certificate of Registration should you ever wish to bring a lawsuit alleging that someone is infringing your copyright.

The Certificate of Registration will serve as proof in a lawsuit that you are the owner of the copyright of the computer program at issue, and also will be evidence of the date of your copyright.

How to Register

Is it difficult to get a Certificate of Registration, and how much does it cost?

It is relatively simple to register a claim to a copyright and get a Certificate of Registration. It costs $10.00. If you have little or no experience in registering a copyright, seek advice from an attorney familiar with both computers and copyright.

The steps for registering a copyright claim are:

1. *Obtain Application Form TX—*
   from Information and Publications Section, LM-455 U.S. Copyright Office:
   Library of Congress,
   Washington, D.C. 20559
   (Tel. 202-287-8700)

2. Fill out Form TX—
   Before filling out Form TX, read carefully the Basic Information Instructions that were received with the form.

   Author—Keep in mind that the term "author" refers to the person who wrote the computer program, unless that person wrote the program as part of his or her regular employment duties in which case the employer is the "author."

   Deposit—The term "deposit" refers to an identifying material, such as a copy of part or all of the computer program, which must be sent in with Form TX and deposited with the Copyright Office to show what is being registered. Concern was expressed about revealing to the public complete copies of computer programs. To meet this concern, the Copyright Office has developed special deposit rules for computer programs and documentation. Special rules are in effect, too, regarding the deposit of machine-readable databases.

   If you have never before filled out a Form TX or put together a copy of all or part of a computer program to serve as a deposit, get advice from an attorney or other knowledgeable person.

3. Mail Form TX, along with identifying material, and $10.00 to the Register of Copyrights, U.S. Copyright Office at the above address.

4. When you receive your Certificate of Registration from the U.S. Copyright Office, put it in a safe place.

Giving Others Notice of Your Copyright

Act immediately to give others notice of your copyright when your computer program is in usable or finished form. Do not wait until you have filed Form TX with the U.S. Copyright Office.

Place a copyright notice on your program, as follows:

© 1986 Jane C. Doe.

This provides notice of the copyright, the year the program was first published, and the name of the copyright owner.

Effect of U.S. Copyright in Foreign Countries

The above exact form of notice is absolutely necessary if you wish your program to be protected in many other countries. About sixty countries adhere to the Universal Copyright Convention, which recognizes the above form of copyright notice. Do not substitute any other shape for the circle around the "c" when the copyright notice is printed on paper or other material that is markable in the normal fashion. However, when the copyright notice is to appear on a computer monitor screen and the computer will not produce a "c" in a circle, the custom has been to use (c) or the word "Copyright." Adding "All Rights Reserved" may provide protection in some Latin American countries.

When Does Copyright Protection Begin?

Theoretically, your computer program is copyrighted from the moment of creation, that is, when it is in fixed and tangible form. However, were you to be challenged in court about the date your copyright protection began, your lawyer would rely on the date your notice of copyright appeared on the computer program and the date on your Certificate of Registration from the U.S. Copyright Office.

Length of Time of Copyright Protection

The term of a copyright is the lifetime of the author, plus fifty years.

After the author's death, rights go to the author's heirs or assigns.

If there are two or more authors, the term is the lifetime of the last surviving author, plus fifty years.

Where to Place a Copyright Notice on a Computer Program

Where should a copyright notice be placed on a computer program?

A copyright notice should appear on the printed label on the floppy disk containing the computer program, on the screen when the program first appears, and anywhere else where users will see the notice.

Remember that the purpose of the copyright notice is to inform others that the program is protected by copyright. Therefore, it is incumbent on the copyright owner to place the copyright notice in reasonable places so as to let people know that there is copyright protection on the program. The purpose of the notice is not to prohibit people from using the program, just to inform them that before using the program they should get permission from the copyright owner. This may or may not involve paying for the program. Sometimes a copyright owner permits use without payment. But the copyright owner never chooses to permit use without permission, unless the owner has placed the program in the public domain for use by anyone.

LEGAL PROTECTION OF COMPUTER PRODUCTS AS TRADE SECRET LAW

May one use trade secret law to protect a computer product, such as a computer program one writes?

Yes.

The problem is that a trade secret must be kept secret or it will lose its protection. Therefore, if you are planning to use your program yourself, and you and a very few trusted colleagues are the only ones who know the secret, it is possible to protect the program as a trade secret. Also, a trade secret can be reverse engineered.

If, however, you plan to sell or license the program widely, you may be better off seeking the protection of a copyright.

LEGAL PROTECTION OF COMPUTER PRODUCTS BY TRADEMARK

Trademark law can be useful in protecting marketable computer products.

A recent case involving trademark is informative, even though it deals with a secret process rather than computer products.

A professor developed a secret process for acidophilus milk, which the university protected by the trademark, "Sweet Acidophilus." The professor sought a share of the royalties from the university's licensing of the process. The court noted that the university's patent policy, which provided for sharing of royalties, was not intended to cover trademarks or trade secrets. The professor alleged the university owed him a fiduciary duty to share the royalties.

The basic problem was to sort out the ownership rights in this intellectual property, which then would determine whether the university owed a fiduciary duty to the professor to share the royalties.

The court found that the professor had been employed specifically to develop such a process. Therefore, said the court, the secret process protected by trademark belonged to the university, not the professor. The university owed the professor no fiduciary duty to share the royalties received.[4]

LEGAL PROTECTION OF COMPUTER PROGRAMS BY PATENT

Is a computer program patentable?

Only rarely, such as where the computer program is part of a patentable process.

In 1981, the U.S. Supreme Court held that it is possible to protect computer programs by patent where the computer program is part

---

[4]Speck v. North Carolina Dairy Foundation, 391 S.E. 2d 139 (1984).

of a patentable process. The specific case involved a patent for a process for curing rubber that incorporated a programmed computer to regulate heat during the curing process.[5]

However, it must be emphasized that it was the total process for curing rubber that was patentable, not the computer program standing alone.

LEGAL PROTECTION OF COMPUTER HARDWARE BY PATENT

Computer hardware, such as keyboards, display screens, disk drives, and blank chips, may be protected by patent.

An application for a patent normally would be prepared with the assistance of a patent attorney. A prototype usually is required.

Each school or college should have a policy concerning ownership and legal protection of computer hardware invented by employees or students.

LEGAL PROTECTION OF MASK WORKS

A semiconductor product may be thought of as containing three parts. There is the chip or silicon wafer itself (hardware). There is the computer program (software). And there is the stencil, known as a masked work, used to make the chip.

In 1984, the Semiconductor Chip Protection Act[6] was passed to create a new form of protection for masked works. This protection is separate and distinct from copyright law. Registration and deposit are required, and failure to register terminates the protection afforded by the act.

The Semiconductor Chip Protection Act established the first new form of statutory intellectual property in the United States in over 100 years. One of the principal goals of the act is to permit the semiconductor industry to combat chip piracy.

RECOMMENDATIONS

Develop and disseminate policies regarding ownership of computer software and hardware created by faculty, administrators, staff, and students.

Develop and disseminate policies regarding support services for commercial exploitation of computer products, especially any contemplated sharing of royalties and revenues.

Make every reasonable effort to assure that individuals are aware of information about ownership and commercial exploitation of work they create before work is begun.

[5]Diamond v. Dieher,[5] 450 U.S. 175 (1981).
[6]Semiconductor Chip Protection Act,[6] 17 U.S.C. Sec. 900.

Chapter V

Liability Related to Employment

As was discussed earlier, one of the principal legal issues faced by educators at schools and colleges concerns legal ownership of computer programs and hardware created by faculty, administrators, and staff members. Contracts of employment often do not deal with the issue of ownership of intellectual property. Therefore, it is becoming essential that each educational institution formulate a policy statement on ownership of computer software and hardware created by faculty, staff, and administrators. In developing policy, a number of factual situations should be kept in mind.

COPYRIGHTS: OWNERSHIP OF SOFTWARE WRITTEN BY EMPLOYEES

Employees often ask, "Do I own the copyright on a computer program I write?" Does it matter whether I write it on the computer at work or on my computer at home?"

There are two schools of thought on the answer to these questions.

Computer programs are defined as literary works. Most schools and colleges appear to be following a trend that treats ownership of copyright of computer programs as they do ownership of other literary works, such as books and articles. Faculty, administrators, and staff who write books and articles usually are considered to be the owners of the copyright to those literary works. Generally, then, the employee would own the copyright on a computer program he or she writes. The exception would be where the employee was hired by the school or college to write computer programs as part of the duties of the job. In that situation, any work-related programs an employee writes would be "work done for hire." Such programs are owned by the employer. In fact, the employer, in such a case, would be considered to be the "author" of the software program, and has the right to copyright it.

An employee may say, "But, I wrote the whole program at home on my own computer and on my own time."

What matters is whether writing the computer program was part of an employee's employment duties.

Suppose an individual was hired as a staff person in admissions. One of her duties was to assist in computerizing the admissions process. It would not matter where or when she wrote software programs for handing admissions. Most likely, creating such admissions programs would be considered part of her job. The admissions programs written by that staff person would belong to her employer, and the employer would have the right to copyright them.

On the other hand, if that same employee received permission to stay after work and use the employer's computer to write non-work-related computer programs, such as for use by the teaching faculty in the English department, or, if she wrote computer programs to handle financial budgeting, she would be in a strong position to assert that those computer programs belonged to her. The individual who wrote them probably would be deemed the author and have the right to copyright them.

The second school of thought on this matter takes the position that under the language of the revised Copyright Act of 1976, scholarly writings, such as that often written by faculty and other employees, now are within the course of employment as anticipated by the statute. Thus, they are "works made for hire" belonging to the employer. Under this reasoning, the institution would own the copyright in all scholarly writings. To overcome this presumption, employees of schools and colleges would be required to negotiate individually and explicitly, as part of their employment agreements, that all their writings belong to them.[1]

Example—Software Written by Faculty Member

Does a computer program written by a faculty member belong to the faculty member or to the institution that employs him or her?

Here is a typical example.

A faculty member is assigned to teach English grammar to students who need remedial training.

The faculty member writes a computer program called "Diagramming Sentences Is Fun and Games," which can be used to drill students in the diagramming of sentences.

A big software company wants to negotiate a license with the faculty member to market the program for use in both high schools and colleges.

---

[1]Simon, T.F. (1982-83) "Faculty writings: Are they 'works made for hire' under the 1976 Copyright Act," Journal of College and University law, 1982-83, Vol. 9, No. 4, pp. 485-513.

The employing educational institution takes the position that the faculty member wrote the software program as part of the regular employment duties, and, therefore, the program belongs to the institution. The faculty member contends that the employment contract speaks only about teaching, not developing computer programs. The faculty member believes the diagramming program belongs to him, or her, not to the institution.

Who is right?

A computer program written by a faculty member probably belongs to the faculty member, unless there is a clear understanding that writing computer programs is a part of the faculty member's job.

General Rule

The general rule is that one who writes a computer program is the author of that program, and owns the copyright. An exception exists where one is an employee hired to write computer programs as part of one's job. Then, the computer program is a "work made for hire," and the employer is considered to be the "author" of the program.

In this situation, the issue is what are the normal duties of one employed as a faculty member? That is, would the writing of computer programs be work normally contemplated to be prepared by an employee within the scope of his or her employment?

In this instance, probably not. Here the writing of computer programs probably would be viewed as would the writing of books or articles, and the copyright would belong to the faculty member.

The situation would be quite different, of course if the employment contract expressly discussed the ownership of computer programs.

Example—Computer Software Written by Non-academic Employee

Does a new computer program written by a non-academic employee, staff or administrator, belong to the employee or to the institution?

Generally, such a new computer program would belong to the staff or administrative employee, unless writing the program was within the scope of employment, or agreed to between the employee and the institution.

Let us suppose that a non-academic staff employee in the computer services center writes a computer program called "Deadbeat," which would be very helpful to the student financial records office in keeping track of delinquent student tuition accounts. In trying to sort out whether "Deadbeat" belongs to the staff employee or the institution, the following issues would need to be addressed. Did the staff employee create "Deadbeat" under the direction and supervision of the employer? Or, did the staff employee simply see the possible need for such a program by education institutions in general, and decide to see what kind of a program she could develop for possible sale to her own employer and to other education institutions?

The controlling factors in determining ownership of the copyrighted work are not necessarily whether or not the staff employee used the employer's time and facilities. What is controlling is whether as part of the employment duties, the employer possessed the right to direct and to supervise the manner in which the work was being performed.

In one case, a court held that the use of a government duplicating machine, government paper, and a government secretary did not make two of Admiral Rickover's speeches "publications of the United States" under the 1909 Copyright Act, Sec. 8.[2]

Software Created Before Employment

Software that relates to one's employment but actually was done prior to the time one began work with the employer belongs to the employee.

Lecture Notes During Employment

Lecture notes belong to the person who wrote them. This is true even if they were written completely on the employer's time, and with the assistance of some of the employer's facilities and personnel.

Working Papers and Drafts

Generally, working papers, false starts, and drafts belong to the employee, absent any express agreement with the employer to the contrary.

"Works Made for Hire"—
Term of Copyright Protection

The term, or length of time, of copyright protection of "works made for hire" is the lesser of:
- Seventy-five years from publication
  or
- One Hundred years from creation.

Note: the term, or length of time, of protection for "works made for hire" is not the same as for other works, i.e. the life of the author plus fifty years.

Transfer of Employee's Copyright to Employer

Sometimes an employer would like to acquire the copyright to a computer program owned by an employee. This may be done simply by affecting a formal transfer of the copyright.

---

[2]See 17 U.S.C. Sec 105. Public Affairs Associates, Inc. v. Rickover, 284 F. 2d 262 (D.C. Cir. 1960); vacated per curiam on other grounds, 369 U.S. 111, 82 S.Ct. 580, 7 L.Ed. 2d 604 (1982); on remand, 268 F. Supp. 444, 452 (D.D.D. 1967).

The transfer from the employee to the employer must be in writing.[3]

The transfer must be recorded with the U.S. Copyright Office either:

- Within one month of the execution of the transfer; or
- Before another transfer is recorded, in order to prevent subsequent purchasers of the copyright who have no knowledge of the transfer from employee to employer from having potentially superior rights.

NONDISCLOSURE AGREEMENT BETWEEN EMPLOYER AND EMPLOYEE

An employer who wishes to protect new work or trade secrets not protected by copyright or patent should have employees sign nondisclosure agreements.

A nondisclosure agreement states that the employee agrees not to disclose confidential information or trade secrets belonging to the employer.

A nondisclosure agreement generally gives examples of what the employer considers confidential or a trade secret, such as: computer program listings, source codes, object codes, information about current works or those under development, and customer lists.

Such an agreement also usually provides that upon termination of employment, the employee agrees to turn over notes, records, and documentation used, created or controlled by the employee during employment.

RESTRICTIVE EMPLOYMENT COVENANTS

There may be times when a educational institution may wish to limit an employee, who has special computer skills, from accepting employment with competing institutions.

For instance, a college may have an employee who specializes in developing computer programs that collect and process information about prospective financial benefactors. The college may wish to protect its advantage in having such computer programs should the particular employee leave its employment.

In drawing up a restrictive employment covenant, the employer must take care not to so restrict the individual's future employment as to deprive the former employee of the ability to make a living as a computer programmer.

In essence, a restrictive employment covenant must be reasonable as to:

The type of work restricted;—

---

[3]17 U.S.C. Sec. 204

The time limit during which the work is restricted; and—

The geographic area in which the work is restricted.[4]

Some states, like California, in effect have outlawed restrictive employment covenants, except in some very narrow areas, for example, where there exists a bona fide "trade secret" or where the sale of a business is involved.

An example of a reasonable restrictive employment covenant in the factual situation mentioned earlier perhaps would be one where the employee's future employment is restricted specifically as a creator of computer programs involving prospective donors to similar colleges, for a one-year period of time, and only at higher education institutions within 100 miles of the employer institution.

Employees Serving "At-Will"

Where employees are serving "at-will," that is, "at the pleasure of the employer," is there ordinarily any form of restrictive employment covenant in effect?

No.

In a case involving at-will employees, a court held that since at-will employees are bound by no restrictive covenants, they may immediately and freely compete with their former employer, including the solicitation of customers.[5]

PERSONAL USE OF EMPLOYER'S COMPUTER

May an employee use an employer's computer for personal business?

An employer may set up policy guidelines to permit an employee to use employer's computer for personal business.

Problems arise when an employer has not informed employees what the policy is regarding personal use of employer's computer.

It is not unusual, for instance, for secretaries who operate word processing computers to "moonlight" by providing secretarial services for faculty, staff, and others, outside their normal working hours. Faculty members may wish to do research or carry on some form of outside business activity, using the institution's computer at odd hours.

An employer should promulgate a clear policy regarding the kind and amount of personal use employees may make of an institution's computer.

An employer may not wish to have certain computer equipment used by employees, especially if that equipment provides potential access to confidential records or data.

---

[4]United States v. Dubilier Condenser Corp., 289 U.S. 178, at 293-294 (1983).
[5]Republic Systems and Programming Inc. v. Computer Assistance, Inc., 322 F. Supp. 619 (D. Conn. 1970), affirmed 440 F. 2d 996 (2nd Cir. 1971).

In one case, an employer did not make clear precisely what kinds of restrictions it placed on an employee's use of the company computer for personal business. An employee used the company computer in connection with his part-time real estate business. The employer discharged him, and maintained he was ineligible for unemployment benefits. A court held that the employee's behavior did not disqualify him for unemployment benefits because the employer's rules were not clear regarding personal use of the company computer.[6]

COMPUTER SOFTWARE WRITTEN BY CONSULTANT OR CONTRACTOR

Schools and colleges often need a new piece of software written for them, and may contract with someone outside the institution to do the work. Does a new computer program written by an independent outsider, such as a consultant or contractor, belong to the outsider or to the institution that hired the outsider?

Generally, the new software belongs to the author, that is, the independent contractor or consultant. If an institution wishes to own the copyright of the new program, it should make sure the contract with the independent contractor or consultant expressly makes that clear, and that the compensation paid for the work reflects the fact that ownership belong to the institution.

Ordinarily, an independent contractor or consultant is not an employee. An independent outsider is hired to provide short-term or one-of-a-kind help in situations where an employer does not want to add another regular employee to the payroll and have to pay Social Security and other benefits. Therefore, the new software program created by an independent outsider would not be a "work made for hire" by an employee within the scope of employment.

An exception to this general rule, where the work would belong to the institution, would be where an independent outsider was hired to produce a "specially commissioned" work. Specially commissioned works would include computer work. Specially commissioned works would include computer sub-routines or programs that are:

- parts of a larger computer program so that they qualify as a "contribution to a collective work."
- "translations," as from one computer language to another, e.g. from COBOL to Fortran.
- enhancements or modifications to an existing computer program, such that they would be considered "supplementary works."
- meant to be merged into a single, integrated package of pre-existing works, and, as such, be a "compilation."
- documentation and considered to be "instructional texts."

---

[6]Giss v. Sumrall, 409 So. 2d 1227 (La. App. 1981).

OWNERSHIP OF COMPUTER HARDWARE INVENTED BY EMPLOYEES

Patenting Computer Hardware

Employers have to deal with legal issues regarding the ownership of new computer hardware invented by employees. An employee policy manual or handbook should state clearly the employer's patent policy.

Ownership of Inventions, Such as Computer Hardware

An employee may ask, "Suppose I invent a new piece of computer hardware. Don't I have the right to patent it?

The general rule is that an employee owns his own inventions and patents, unless he agreed they would belong to his employer.

In the academic world, a tradition exists regarding the patenting of inventions and discoveries of faculty and other employees. It is that employees usually assign rights in their patents to their employing institutions, and the revenue received from the license or sale of the invention is shared between the faculty member and the institution. The formula for sharing may be based on a sliding scale or whatever way is agreed upon by the parties.

Even if an employee did not turn over patent rights to his employer, the theory of "shop rights" may apply. Under the theory of shop rights, an employee may patent the invention, but an employer has a perpetual, royalty-free license to use it.

RECOMMENDATIONS

It is particularly important that employees, such as faculty, administrators, and staff, are given clear information about an employer's position regarding:

- ownership of newly created computer software or hardware;
- support services provided by the employer for commercial exploitation; and—
- possible sharing of royalties and other revenues.

Where an employer has trade secrets, employees should be informed about the need for confidentiality and asked to sign confidentiality agreements.

Where one wishes to discuss with others, one's trade secrets or other confidential information about new software or hardware, consider asking others to sign a non-disclosure agreement prior to the discussion.

Develop rules to govern employees' use of the employer's computer equipment, particularly use for personal business.

Employees, especially those who do programming, should be informed about the possible need for personal liability insurance.

It may be helpful for an employer to provide an office or an institutional representative to whom employees may go with questions.

Chapter VI

Liability Related to Students

STUDENTS WHO CREATE COMPUTER PROGRAMS
General Rule

Educators at schools and colleges may be asked: Does a student own a computer program he or she creates? The answer is: Generally, yes, but not always.

Students' legal relationship with their institution usually is based on their contract of enrollment. There is usually little or nothing in a contract of enrollment that would entitle an institution to ownership of a student's work.

Under the Copyright Act, a computer program is copyrighted automatically as soon as it is in tangible, fixed form. This means that a flow chart, as well as the final form of the program, is copyrighted as soon as it is in tangible, fixed form. Therefore, as soon as a student creates a flow chart or a final program, the work is copyrighted, and the student owns the copyright.

This is so because ordinarily the person who creates a computer program is considered to be the "author" of the program; and the author owns the copyright. Then, a student would own the copyright.

Student as Employee of Institution

There could be conditions under which a student who created a computer program would not be considered the "author." For instance, a student may be hired or commissioned by an institution specifically to develop a computer program for the institution. The program, then, would be a "work made for hire," and the "author" would be the institution. The institution would own the copyright from the moment of creation of the work.

Student Software as Class Assignment

A more troublesome instance would be where a student creates a computer program as one of the assignments for a course, or as a project meeting the academic requirements for a graduate degree.

Educational institutions only recently have begun developing policies to deal with the growing number of situations where students write computer programs which prove to be valuable commercially, such as games or business or educational applications programs.

A situation of this nature between a student and an institution usually is viewed as one involving ethical considerations as well as purely legal considerations. The relationship between a student and an institution generally is rather one-sided, with most of the power residing in the institution. Therefore, care must be taken to treat students in these situations in an authentically fair and open fashion. No institution wants to develop a reputation for using "sharp practices" in its dealing with students.

Institutional Control Over Student's Creation of Software

Where a school or college wishes to claim ownership of student works created to meet academic requirements, the institution should set forth explicitly in the students' contracts of enrollment and in the institution's documents, such as, its admissions materials, its governing board policies, its student handbook, its course descriptions and its degree requirements in its catalogue, or in other similar documents— that in academic matters the institution has the right to give students direction and supervision, through its faculty and staff, such that all work created by students to meet academic requirements belongs to the institution. When such steps have been taken and a computer program is created by a student as part of the academic work required for a course or degree, the institution could take the position that the institution was the true "author" of that program and owned the copyright. The institution might then sell or license the computer program, and share the revenues with the student, perhaps in the form of tuition credit.

The above student/institution situation would be analogous to an employee/institution situation in which a court has held that:

The essential factor in determining whether an employee created his work of art within the scope of his employment as part of his employment duties is whether the employer possessed the right to direct and to supervise the manner in which the work was being performed.[1]

The **Scherr** court went on to say that:

Other pertinent, but nonessential, considerations are those indicating at whose insistence, expense, time and facilities the work was created.[2]

---

[1]Scherr v. Universal Match Corp., 417 F. 2d 497, at 500, 164 U.S.P.Q. 225, U.S. Court of Appeals for the Second Circuit, 1969.
[2]Scherr, supra, at 500-501.

Student Software Created in Spare Time

A growing number of students create computer programs in their off-hours, that is, on their own time and not for course credit. A student may or may not use some of the institution's facilities, such as its computer. Again, to call upon an employment analogy, the student probably owns the computer program created. See *Public Affairs Associates, Inc.* v. *Rickover,*[1] where the court held that use of a government duplicating machine, government paper and a government secretary did not make two of Admiral Rickover's speeches "publications of the United States" under the 1909 Copyright Act[2].

The above situation has been dealt with by some institutions by asking students to compensate the institution for the cost of the use of institutional equipment, such as a computer. However, this poses problems since students may have paid tuition for general use of institutional equipment. Also, it is not at all uncommon for such institutional equipment as athletic, theater, art, and laboratory equipment to be used freely by students in off hours.

RECOMMENDATIONS

Develop and disseminate policies regarding ownership of computer software or hardware created by students.

Inform students about any possible support services for commercial exploitation.

Make clear to students whether any sharing of royalties or other revenues is expected.

Help students understand the need for legal protection of their work, including their asking others to sign confidentiality agreements before revealing their work to others.

Help students understand the possible need for programmers to have personal liability insurance.

Provide an office or individual to answer students' questions.

---

[1]Public Affairs Associates, Inc. v. Rickover, 284 F. 2d 262 (D.C. Cir. 1960); vacated per curiam on other grounds, 369 U.S. 111, 82 S.Ct. 580, 7 L.Ed. 2d 604 (1962); on remand, 268 F. Supp. 444, 452 (D. D.C. 1967)

[2]1909 Copyright Act, Sec. 8. See 17 U.S.C. Sec. 105.

Chapter VII

Liability for Negligence

INCORRECT COMPUTERIZED RECORDS

Most schools and colleges have offices that perform various record keeping functions where there is a potential for error, such as student admissions and records, personnel, and business services.

Is an institution liable for damage or injury caused by incorrect computerized records?

Very likely.

It is becoming increasingly clear that a school or college that relies on incorrect computerized records and thereby causes an injury may find that it is liable under tort theory.

Because records that are computerized tend to be intimidating, some staff members appear to be reluctant to listen to or act upon proffered correct information.

Take the instance of student financial records at post-secondary institutions. A student may be threatened with expulsion or suspension due to an alleged delinquent tuition payment. The student may bring in a cancelled check to show that the computerized record probably is incorrect. The staff in the financial records office may be reluctant to act, mainly because there is no clear and simple mechanism available to allow corrections easily of the computerized records. Were a student to be able to show damages resulting from this set of facts, tort liability may accrue to the institution.

Something similar could occur regarding the forwarding of an incorrect academic transcript, or an incorrect personnel record.

An example of such a tort claim arose in a non-academic setting. An auto credit company relied upon incorrect computerized records with regard to payments for the purchase of a car. The car purchaser offered correct information to the company, but the company persisted in its error and repossessed the car. A Missouri court ordered both actual and punitive damages.[1]

In a case decided by the Supreme Court in 1985, a credit reporting agency sent five subscribers a false report that a contractor had filed a voluntary petition for bankruptcy. The contractor sued the credit agency, alleging libel. The contractor sought presumed and punitive damages. The Supreme Court was asked to rule on the issue of whether the contractor had to prove that the credit agency acted with "actual malice." The Supreme Court held that the contractor did not have to show "actual malice" in order to recover.[2]

IMPROPERLY PROGRAMMED COMPUTER

An improperly programmed computer could cause damages for which an institution may be held liable.

Computers often are blamed for the mistakes of the human beings who program or operate them. Granted, there are occasions when a computer itself makes an error, usually due to an electrical surge or similar glitch. More common is a situation where the person doing the programming, or the person responsible for seeing that the programming was done correctly, simply was not careful enough.

Let us imagine that a student handbook provides that where a student is drunk in class, he is subject to possible suspension or expulsion after a due process hearing. Let us further suppose that the handling of student disciplinary cases have been "computerized." However, the computer programmer forgot to program the computer to send out appropriate due process information concerning notice of the charge and opportunity for a hearing prior to declaring the student suspended or expelled. The institution may be liable for deprivation of due process, and may not be permitted to rely on the excuse that its computer was not properly programmed.

In a case involving a public gas utility, an appellate court found that the due process termination notice, given to the utility's customers prior to their gas being turned off, was inadequate because of an improperly programmed computer. Here, the court held this violated customers' Fourteenth Amendment due process rights. The court ordered the gas company to follow in the future the court's precise instructions as to the content and timing of service termination notices.[3]

ELECTRONIC BULLETIN BOARDS

Questions of possible legal liability surround the use of computer bulletin boards, a high-tech version of the supermarket bulletin board

---

[1]Price v. *Ford Motor Credit Co.*, 530 S.W. 2d 249, Missouri Court of Appeals, 1975.
[2]Dun & Bradstreet, Inc. v. Greenmoss Builders, Inc., No. 83-18, U.S. Supreme Court, June 16, 1985, 53 U.S.L.W. 4866.
[3]Palmer v. Columbia Gas of Ohio, Inc., 479 F. 2d 153 (1973).

where people advertise services and goods for sale and pass along other messages. For example, would a school or college be liable for negligence if bulletin boards located on their computers contained information that harmed others? Or, if criminal activity were involved, would they be guilty of aiding and abetting?

Electronic bulletin boards are set up by computer users, generally to exchange, via computer, information about new programs, documentation, databases and other matters of special interest to users.

Legal problems arise when, among other information, there appear on electronic bulletin boards items such as: telephone credit card numbers; methods of breaking into corporate, hospital, or government computers; copyrighted software programs; and bank account numbers.

In 1984 an individual was charged with a misdemeanor when his home computer bulletin board was found to contain telephone credit card numbers obtained without authorization. Police seized his personal computer and data storage devices. He was accused of knowingly and willfully publishing telephone credit card numbers with intent they be used to avoid the charges. His defense was that the numbers were published by someone else and that he did not knowingly publish them. The case still is not concluded.[1]

Electronic bulletin boards are being monitored now by telephone companies, government authorities, and software companies, among others.

Schools and colleges would be well advised to attempt to monitor regularly, bulletin boards at their institutions. Enlisting the services of student computer "hackers" to assist in the monitoring could be very helpful.

Illegal, obscene or abusive messages should be removed. When misbehaving individuals are located, appropriate penalties should be assessed.

HEALTH AND SAFETY HAZARDS

Video Display Terminals

Eye problems are reported by persons who work before video display terminals (VDTs). Complaints include: headaches, blurring of vision, itching and burning eyes, eye fatigue, flickering sensations, shooting pains and double vision. The American Optometric Association is instructing its members on how to diagnose and treat the new ills associated with advanced computer technology.[2]

Shock Hazards

Shock hazards sometimes are discovered. One company, Texas Instruments, Inc. reported the remote possibility of a transformer fail-

---

[1] The New York Times, November 12, 1984, p. 1, col. 1.
[2] Buffalo News, July 7, 1983, p. B-7

ure resulting in electric shocks to users and damage to the computer regarding their model 99-4A. The company placed large ads in newspapers to warn of the possible danger. This kind of public announcement is both rare and commendable.[1]

Radiation

Radiation emitted from terminals is being studied as a possible danger for pregnant operators. No conclusive results have been published to date, according to recent information.

References
1. *VDT Risks Program*, 9 to 5 National Association of Working Women, 1224 Huron Road, Cleveland, Ohio, 44115.
2. *VDTs In the Workplace: A Study of the Effects on Employment.* 1984. Washington, D.C.: The Bureau of National Affairs, Inc.
3. *Towards a More Humanized Technology: Exploring the Impact of Video Display Terminals on the Health and Working Conditions of Canadian Office Workers.* 1982. Canadian Labour Education and Studies Centre, 2841 Riverside Drive, Suite 301, Ottawa, Ontario, K1V 8N4, Canada.

Wrongful Death

There have been several instances of computer-related wrongful deaths. Two examples follow.

First, in a very unusual case, a court found that the death of a computer systems supervisor was job related so as to sustain an award of death benefits under a worker's compensation law. An employee who worked as a cashier was promoted to office manager and given supervisory responsibility over seven other employees and a computer system. The worker put in long hours both in the office and at home studying the lengthy computer system operations manual. The worker often arrived home from work exhausted, and yet continued to carry office work home. It happened that this individual had a history of systemic lupus erythematosus, an inflammation of the skin and connective tissues throughout the body, dating back several years. Soon the employee was hospitalized, her condition continued to deteriorate, and she died several months later.

The employee's survivors asked for death benefits under the state worker's compensation statute, and the employer appealed. The court found that while the work itself "did not cause the underlying disease, 'it is very probable . . . that the stress, effort, and chronic fatigue incident to her . . . death was an important factor in precipitating an acute exacerbation (and) systemic spread of the condition, (and) hastened, excited and accelerated' the employee's death." The appeals court

---

[1]Buffalo News, February 23, 1983, p.A-6.

A second example involved a worker on an assembly line who was killed by a robotic arm. The legal liability in this case is not yet determined.

These examples point to the need for monitoring of the physical well-being of individuals working with computers as well as the need for monitoring the mechanical maintenance of computer machinery.

RECOMMENDATIONS

Inform employees about legal liability possible as a result of any injury or damages caused by incorrect computerized records, improperly programmed computers, or unauthorized information on electronic bulletin boards.

Take reasonable steps to provide safe and healthful working conditions where computer equipment is involved.

Be especially aware of dangers from fire at computer sites, particularly dangers from toxic fumes.

Chapter 8

Liability Resulting from Inadequate Computer Security

Liability may arise as a result of poor security planning and lack of implementation of appropriate countermeasures to threats to computers.

Computer systems require protection against both attacks and failures. There are a number of security measures that should be considered in protecting computers from either accidental or deliberate threats. When security measures fail, the losses in time and money may be substantial. There may be a loss of availability of the computer, such that service cannot be provided as scheduled or at all. There may be a loss of integrity, such that the computer no longer performs properly. There may be a loss of confidentiality, such that unauthorized persons have access to data. There also may be a loss of data or of monies.

To take care of those situations where security measures do not prevent attacks or failure, there need to be contingency plans to handle whatever eventuates.

Risk management, especially adequate insurance coverage, is essential.

PRIVACY AND CONFIDENTIALITY

Schools and colleges have a special concern to protect the privacy and confidentiality of their records and research data.

It is well recognized that educational institutions are constrained by certain privacy statutes. The federal Family Educational Rights and Privacy Act of 1974 (FERPA), known as the Buckley Amendment, provides for privacy of student academic records by permitting access only by the student and certain authorized persons.[1]

---

[1] Family Educational Rights and Privacy Act, 20 U.S.C. Section 1232g (1976 & Supp. V, 1981).

Educators have asked whether the practice of computerizing record keeping has made it impossible to meet the confidentiality requirements of laws such as the Buckley Amendment.

Computer experts point out that confidentiality of computerized records and data can be maintained in several ways.

Access codes can be used in connection with computerized record keeping, in order to provide confidentiality on the one hand and appropriate access on the other.

Access codes will protect certain "fields of information so that only authorized persons are able to reach certain information. For instance, a record clerk may be given an access code that will permit seeing a person's name, address, and any other information relevant to the clerk's job. But that access code may not enable the clerk to see academic grades, or, perhaps, certain financial information about a particular student or employee.

Research data, likewise can be protected by the use of access codes or by encryption devices.

In addition, some institutions use three separate computer systems, unconnected by telephone or other similar communication, for the institution's business records, its research data, and its teaching materials.

Identifier numbers are another matter often brought to the attention of legal counsel. In general, it is a wise idea not to use social security numbers as identifiers. Under the provisions of statutes such as the federal Privacy Act[1] and the Social Security Act,[2] individuals may have the option of not revealing their social security number. An institution that refuses to recognize such an option may be in violation of the law.[3]

PHYSICAL SECURITY

Liability for negligence in caring for computer equipment and personnel is an issue that requires some discussion. There are foreseeable injuries to computer equipment and personnel that require reasonable preventive measures to be taken.

To mention just a few examples, reasonable steps should be taken to prevent injury and damage due to:

- unauthorized access to a computer site, whether it is a building or a room;
- heat and dust, due to poor air conditioning;
- smoke and fire;
- water, including floods.

---

[1]Privacy Act, 5 U.S.C. Section 552a and note (1982).
[2]Social Security Act, 42 U.S.C. Section 405(c)(2)(C)(i, iii) (1976 & Supp. V, 1981).
[3]Doyle v. Wilson, 529 F. Supp. 1343, U.S. District Court for the District of Delaware, 1982.

The physical security of computers is largely dependent on the locale and design and construction of the building in which the computer is housed.

Where a new building is being built, consideration can be given to a number of important environmental factors, such as whether there are chemical plants nearby emitting harmful fumes, whether the ground is solid, whether electrical storms are frequent, and what the risks are regarding floods, wind, and ice.

Where an old building is being renovated, there may be very little opportunity to avoid such risks.

In either case, building materials used should be of the kind that do not emit dangerous fumes when warm or burning.

Computers placed above ground level can be better protected from flooding. Where computers must be placed below ground level, pumps and similar devices should be provided.

Emergency exit doors should be plainly marked and well known.

Electrical power supply is a paramount importance. There should be a backup power supply in case the main power supply is interrupted.

Electrical power line filtering devices are helpful in avoiding damage that can be done by surges, spikes or "noise" that may occasionally occur in your source of electrical energy.

Air conditioning will probably be a must for most uses of computers. Proper ventilation is required to maintain appropriate humidity and temperature, and dust must be kept to a minimum.

Static electricity can erase data from disks, so floor coverings should be anti-static to whatever degree possible.

Outside, a wall surrounding the building but away from it should help discourage intruders and vandals. This creates a "safety moat" around a building. Obviously, this is an extreme security measure that may be appropriate only in a few instances.

Controlling Access to Computer, Room or Building

First, for any controlled access system to be effective, it must be viewed as valuable by the people involved. Without the cooperation of human beings, almost any access control system can be breached. Therefore, one of the most important steps in setting up a controlled access system is to make clear to people why it is important. Obvious reasons include the physical safety of personnel and equipment from vandals and even terrorists.

Second, the institution must make clear how important it considers the access control system to be, and what penalties and sanctions will be applied for nonadherence to the access rules.

As for methods of restricting access, computer security experts often refer to three basic ways:

- controls using people;

- controls using mechanical locks; and
- controls using electronic systems.

People, such as secretaries and security guards, may be used to screen and challenge persons seeking access to a computer. Authorized persons may be identified by placing their names on a list, or by issuing passes or badges. Whoever is serving as a checker must be trained carefully as to what to do if help is needed.

Mechanical locks using conventional keys may be helpful but are circumvented easily. They are, of course, better than nothing.

Electronic systems often use card keys and key pads, singly or in combination, to control access. These, too, can be circumvented, but not as easily as mechanical locks.

Another form of electronic access control involves wearing a small, electronic transmitter that, in turn, controls locks.

From time to time, security systems need to be changed or updated to decrease the likelihood that persons will become so familiar with the system that they learn to circumvent it easily.

Controlling Access to Software

Liability for damage done to software programs and data stored in computers can be significant.

Passwords and other code words often are used to control access to computer programs.

Both operating system programs and applications programs need to be protected by reasonable means. Damage to or loss of operating system software can shut down completely any use of a computer. Damage to or loss of applications programs can halt whatever particular service depends on the applications programs, such as accounting services, payroll services, registration of students, record keeping of grades, library services, or collection and analysis of research data.

Operating system security measures may be built right into the system by the manufacturer, or they may be added on later. One school of thought is that if the operating system security measures are built right into the system, then any systems programmer may be able to evade them, though other staff members may have a harder time doing so. An add-on security system, on the other hand, may be known only to a very select group of persons so that it is harder to evade by all concerned.

The access control system for software should:
- identify every user;
- maintain access controls over data, programs, processes, and resources, so that only authorized users can access them in authorized ways;

- maintain a log of all use, including alerting staff of attempted breach of the security rules; and
- be secure, so that security checks cannot be evaded, and the log cannot be changed.

A number of companies specialize in developing secure operating systems. They can be costly and cumbersome. The costs and benefits of such security packages must be weighed carefully.

This is a field in which expert advice must be sought.

RECOMMENDATIONS

Carefully select and train employees and other users of computer equipment.

Explain to employees and students the importance of maintaining privacy and confidentiality of certain computerized records.

Review and monitor regularly the security arrangements for computer sites, equipment and data.

Have contingency and recovery plans to handle situations involving breach of computer security or damage to equipment, including backups for software and standbys for hardware.

Chapter IX

Computer Crime

Crimes involving the use of computers can cost schools and colleges substantial sums of money. Institutions should inform faculty, staff, administrators and students what the institution's policy is regarding prosecution of criminal activities. Perpetrators must be prepared to face both external and campus penalties.

Fraud, embezzlement, theft, trespass, invasion of privacy, physical damage to equipment and information, and extortion are among the more standard crimes connected to the use of computers. In addition, two other crimes need to be mentioned as matters of special interest. They are: unauthorized use of computers and the interstate transportation of stolen intellectual property.

FEDERAL COMPUTER CRIME STATUTES

Congress recently passed two federal statutes aimed at criminal acts involving computers. They are the Federal Comprehensive Crime Act of 1984 and the Counterfeit Access Device and Computer Fraud and Abuse Act of 1984. These statutes make almost all computer-related fraud, theft, tampering or destruction a federal offense.

STATE COMPUTER CRIME STATUTES

At least nineteen states had computer crime statutes on their books as of September 1984. They are: Alaska, Arizona, California, Colorado, Delaware, Florida, Georgia, Illinois, Michigan, Minnesota, Missouri, Montana, New Mexico, North Carolina, Ohio, Rhode Island, Utah, Virginia, and Wisconsin. Legislation was about to be passed also in Hawaii, Massachusetts, and New York.

Examples

Computer crimes are characterized in present legislation as:
- deceiving a machine;
- computer fraud (with and without intent to deceive);

- altering computerized credit information;
- computer damage or destruction;
- offenses against computer users;
- unauthorized use;
- modification or destruction of programs or data;
- use of computer to commit: embezzlement, fraudulent disposition of personal property, larceny, larceny by conversion;
- tampering or alteration of computer;
- unauthorized access;
- denial of computer services;
- altering or destroying programs;
- computer trespass—removing data, causing malfunction, alter, create, or erase data;
- extortion via threats to damage computer;
- theft of computer-related materials;
- theft of computer services;
- computer invasion of privacy—unauthorized examination of personal or financial data;
- personal trespass by computer, cause physical injury;
- offenses against computer data programs;
- offenses against computer equipment and supplies;

Penalties range from ninety days to twenty years of imprisonment, and from $100 to $150,000 + in fines.

UNAUTHORIZED USE OF COMPUTERS

The unauthorized use of a computer is perhaps the most common computer crime on campus. Typical examples include: (1) a student logging on in order to gain some extra skill in computer use; (2) a faculty member logging on in order to do some non-work-related personal business; and (3) the person who wishes to damage or alter data or other information stored in the computer.

Along with a wide range of unauthorized uses, there are degrees of intent to do mischief. An educational institution must have a policy for how it will respond to varying degrees and types of unauthorized use. Its response may range from a slap on the wrist to the filing of a criminal charge.

Regarding criminal prosecution, it was not a simple matter to prosecute for unauthorized access to a computer in the days when there was no specific language to cover such behavior in a criminal code. An early unsuccessful prosecution in 1977 involved a graduate student's unauthorized use of a university computer in order to complete the research necessary for his doctoral dissertation. In that instance, faculty members responsible for his getting authorized access to the computer apparently failed to make the necessary arrangements. The student simply took matters into his own hands, found a way to learn the proper access code to log on to the computer, and used computer time which he billed to various university accounts. The student was charged with larceny under the Virginia Criminal Code. Ultimately, a court held the unauthorized use of the computer here was not a larceny because of the particular wording of relevant portions of the Virginia Code.[1]

Now, many states have modified their criminal codes in order to make unauthorized use of a computer a crime. So, an institution needs to examine its own state's criminal code before writing its policy regarding how it will respond to unauthorized use of its computer.

INTERSTATE TRANSPORTATION OF STOLEN INTELLECTUAL PROPERTY

An interesting legal question arose as to whether stolen intellectual property, such as copyrighted material, is the kind of property intended to be included in the coverage of the National Stolen Property Act.[2]

This issue appears to be on its way to being settled by the courts. A federal appellate court held that the interstate transportation of stolen intellectual property, which in this case was unauthorized copies of copyrighted motion pictures, is a violation of the National Stolen Property Act.[3]

Schools and colleges should keep in mind, therefore, that federal jurisdiction may be available where a state statute provides inadequate protection to the institution regarding stolen intellectual property.

RECOMMENDATIONS

Make available information about federal and state penalties for violations of computer crime statutes.

Develop and disseminate policies on internal discipline as well as external criminal and civil prosecution for violations of rules and laws.

Follow your own rules and procedures.

---

[1] Lund v. Commonwealth, 232 S.E. 2d 745, Virginia Supreme Court 1977.
[2] National Stolen Property Act. 18 U.S.C. Sections 2311-2319 (1982).
[3] U.S. v. Belmont, 26 BNA's Patent, Trademark & Copyright Journal, 471 (1983).

Chapter X

Insurance

Any plan for risk management relies heavily on insurance.

Schools and colleges will want to ascertain what insurance coverage is available to cover losses due to:

- damage to computers, programs, and data;
- loss of business;
- injury to and by personnel.

PROPERTY INSURANCE

Property insurance is one answer. However, any property insurance policy should be combined with an on-going practice of making back-up copies of everything, and with a system of protection against electrical surges.

One kind of insurance coverage for business computers can be purchased as part of general business insurance. A common example of general business insurance would be an "all risks" policy that covers the insured for all risks except those specifically excluded. Generally, this would cover against accidental damage caused by: fire, water, storm damage, explosion, theft, malfunction of other equipment, vandalism, and perhaps malicious damage.

Another kind of coverage is a special computer insurance policy that specifically may cover computers, terminals, peripherals, programs, data, and storage media. There also is coverage available for computers while in transit from one site to another.

Special attention should be paid to insurance coverage for software programs and data. For example, ask whether the insurance will pay only to replace blank floppy disks, or will pay the cost of reentering the data on the disks. Ask also whether the insurance covers floods, earthquakes, and mechanical and electrical breakdown. Also, does it cover data erasure by magnet or electricity? And what about programming errors?

PERSONAL LIABILITY INSURANCE

Programmers should consider personal liability insurance that covers material loss resulting from errors in a program, or omission of data from a program or database.

HOME COMPUTER INSURANCE

If a computer is used only for home purposes, such as games and hobbies, a homeowner's policy or renter's policy may provide protection. This may involve paying an additional premium to your insurance company for a "floater," "rider," or "endorsement" to your policy to cover the computer.

If, however, a computer is used for work, even at home, it may be defined for insurance purposes as a "business machine" and the insurance company will not pay full replacement value, but only depreciated value.

RECOMMENDATIONS

Review and update present property and personal liability insurance.

Monitor conditions to keep track of possible changes requiring modifications of insurance coverage.

View risk management as including: periodic updating seminars for administrators and supervisors about legal liabilities; competent training of computer users; and proper maintenance of computer equipment and facilities.

Chapter XI

Legal-Ethical Issues

There are certain occasions when a school or college feels obliged to respond to situations in a different manner than other organizations. These times usually are when a particular situation involves a combined legal-ethical matter. More often than not, students are involved. There also are a number of legal-ethical situations regarding faculty, staff and administrators.

ABUSE OF STUDENTS AND OTHER VULNERABLE PERSONS

First of all, how should an institution respond when a student is abused in connection with the use of computers?

Should not an institution come down hard on the perpetrators of abuse of students in such situations?

For example, a faculty member or a graduate teaching assistant may tell a student who has computer skills that unless the student assists in getting unauthorized access to certain data or free computer time, the student will receive a poor or failing grade. Or, a supervising faculty member may tell a graduate student who is trying to finish research needed to complete a dissertation that unless the graduate student helps to break into another faculty member's research database, the faculty supervisor will delay progress on the graduate student's dissertation.

These are unethical and unconscionable pressures. A school or college must deal with them strongly.

ABUSE OF COMPUTERS BY STUDENTS

When a student breaks the code of a computer what should be the institution's response? Should the response to a student's act be different from the response to a faculty or staff member's act?

There are a wide range of responses possible, and it is up to the institution, usually, whether it responds differently to computer abuse done by students compared to that done by faculty or staff.

Breaking the code of a school or college computer is a fairly common activity. Sometimes it is done as a prank, while at other times the breaking of the code may be for some criminal purpose, such as embezzling funds. At still other times, there may be conduct falling somewhere in between, that is, breaking a code in order to change a grade or plagiarize some information or work.

An educational institution has to determine in advance what range of responses it chooses to have available in such situations. It must then make sure to inform students, faculty, staff and others what its policies are regarding computer abuse. If there are potential violations of a state computer crime statute involved, the institution would want to inform students about the statute, what it defines as computer crime, and what the penalties are as to possible imprisonment and fines. Finally, the institution must follow whatever procedures it has said it would follow in instances of computer abuse.

For example, where a student is involved in what is clearly intended as a prank, the institution may wish to respond as it would to other student pranks. At the other extreme, where a student is involved in an activity that clearly is intended as a criminal act, the institution may have little choice but to react much more severely.

An ethical dimension is added to issues of student abuse incidents by the tradition on campus of tending to view a student as a person still going through a learning process, and, therefore, not always being held as accountable as would be the case in some other setting. Exactly how an institution views abuses of computers should be made known to all in advance, as mentioned above. School and college policies and handbooks should make plain which kinds of computer offenses are considered minor offenses and which will be considered serious offenses, and should indicate what different penalties then may be applied. As has just been noted, the intent of the student may make a difference, and could in some instances mitigate the circumstances.

It should be made clear that abuse of computers, however mild, does do some form of damage to computer equipment, data, or other persons, and that some form of punitive response should be expected.

When abuse of computers is the work of nonstudents, such as faculty or other staff members, the same ethical concerns may not apply. Special consideration may be given to students on the basis of the tradition that students are persons still going through a learning process, such that their mistakes may be viewed as part of the learning process. That is not the case with nonstudents. Faculty, staff, and administrators are placed in roles requiring them to supervise students and set examples for students. Therefore, faculty, staff, and administrators often are to be held to a higher standard of behavior than are students.

INSTITUTION'S RESPONSIBILITY TO PROTECT DATA AND RECORDS STORED IN COMPUTERS

A school or college has a responsibility, ethically and legally, to take reasonable steps to protect data and records stored in its computers.

Sometimes it takes no more than a telephone call from a local newspaper reporter to a clerk in an admissions and records office to learn the grades of almost any student there. This has been known to happen regarding inquiries by sports reporters concerning the grades and academic standing of basketball and football players as they relate to eligibility to participate in certain games.

Revealing a student's grades to unauthorized persons is, of course, a violation of the Family Educational Rights and Privacy Act of 1974 (Buckley Amendment) which protects the privacy of students' academic records.

Similarly, a clerk in a personnel office may be asked to reveal certain financial information about faculty or staff salaries to unauthorized persons, such as a bank or a department store.

Such problems usually arise where clerks have not been advised as to what kinds of information may be released, or they have not been given a set of procedures to follow when confronted with such requests.

Generally, supervisors have the responsibility for seeing that security procedures for records and other institutional data and property are developed and followed carefully, including making sure that subordinates have been adequately trained to use the procedures.

ACCESS TO COMPUTERS

Schools and colleges generally have latitude to provide whatever training or access to the use of computers by students and others that they choose. But where training or access is promised it must be delivered.

It is well-established that where, for example, a college catalogue or a person in authority, such as a dean, states that certain courses will include hands-on experience using specific equipment, for instance a computer, there is a contractual obligation to provide such experience. A court ordered the refund of tuition in a case in which a catalogue promised hands-on experience with specific welding equipment, but the equipment was not provided.[1] This is similar to the con-

[1]Dizick v. Umpqua Community College, 599 P. 2d 444, Oregon Supreme Court, 1979.

tractual obligation to provide specific courses, faculty, and facilities set forth in a catalogue.

In addition to the contractual obligation described, there also may be an ethical consideration as well. An educational institution may take the position that equity demands that it do its utmost to see that training and access to computers is made available to various of its constituencies. Computer literacy should be available to elementary, secondary, and post-secondary students. At colleges, computer literacy should be accessible not only to its computer science and engineering majors, but to liberal arts majors and others who may be less likely to see, immediately, the importance of computer literacy.

FACULTY EMPLOYMENT AND
THE DEVELOPMENT OF COMPUTER PROGRAMS

Legal-ethical issues affect faculty employment. Copyright protection begins from the moment of creation of the work by its author. As mentioned previously, when a faculty member develops a computer program, the question of its ownership arises. The question may be answered by examining the employment relationship between the faculty member and the institution.

If a faculty member is hired specifically to teach computer programming, it well may be that the job description includes an obligation to develop computer programs as part of the normal employment activities expected. In that situation, new computer programs could be considered "works made for hire." The employer, which in this case is the school or college, would be considered to be the "author" of the computer programs, and would own the programs along with the copyright.

If, on the other hand, a faculty member is employed to fulfill the normal duties expected of a faculty person, which at the college level might include teaching, research and service, and the faculty person's discipline is, for instance, biology, then a computer program developed by the faculty person to handle large scale voter surveys probably would not be the property of the institution.

Between the two extremes described above are a great variety of possible scenarios.

What is advisable is that a school or college try to anticipate situations such as those above and others one can imagine easily, and come to some agreement at the time the employment contract is negotiated as to how ownership of intellectual property will be handled.

There are available a number of models of how institutions could handle ownership of intellectual property, such as computer programs. Some examples of models would be:
  • the faculty member owns the computer program and licenses it to the institutions for use or marketing;

- the faculty member transfers ownership of the computer program to the institution;
- the institution hired the faculty member to create computer programs, in which case the programs would be deemed to be "works made for hire" and the institution would be considered to be the "author" and owner of the copyright. The institution generally would share royalties in some fashion with the employee who created the program; or
- the institution could commission a faculty member to create a computer program for the institution, and negotiate terms regarding ownership of copyright and sharing of revenues.

From an ethical standpoint, neither the faculty member nor the school or college in such a situation should take undue advantage of the other. Nor should either party wait until the other is at an unexpected disadvantage to bring up the question of ownership of intellectual property.

One example of a situation involving intellectual property arose between a faculty member and a university concerning confidences given to the university by the faculty member relating to his discovery of a secret process. The university claimed sole ownership of the trademark on the secret process. The faculty member alleged there was a fiduciary relationship existent that prevented sole ownership by the university. The lower court held in favor of the faculty member, but the appeals court found in favor of the university. The appeals court said the faculty member had been hired to do the type of research that led to the secret process, so it belonged to the university.[1]

A clear understanding of ownership rights set forth in an employment contract can largely prevent such legal and ethical uncertainties.

ETHICAL RESPONSIBILITIES AT THE INSTITUTIONAL / DEPARTMENTAL / FACULTY LEVEL

A number of ethical issues arise from the fact that private industry is being attracted more and more to educational institutions as resources for research and development activities. Let us suppose that a corporation wishes to provide funds for the support of certain activities within a school or college in connection with the development of computer equipment and programs.

What kind of ethical responsibilities does the institution have to assure that such generosity flowing to certain activities will not deflect the institution from its overall long-range goals? Collegial mechanisms must be utilized to maintain a balance between the opportunities presented for certain localized institutional development and the overall stated mission of the institution.

---

[1]Speck v. North Carolina Dairy Foundation, 319 S.E. 2d 139 (1984).

For example, sometimes specific faculty members are designated as the recipients of industrial funds to do computer-related research. What happens when a faculty person receives substantial amounts of outside funding and is permitted to hire extra secretaries and assistants and to purchase special equipment? What ethical responsibility has the school or college to assure that other members of the department understand that their particular lines of research and areas of interest are still of importance to the institution and the department?

UNKNOWN PHYSICAL DANGERS

A broad ethical concern exists regarding certain physical dangers that are as yet unclear as they relate to computers.

One highly publicized health question is whether video display terminals (VDTs) emit dangerous radiation. This is of concern not only regarding computer operators who work directly in an employer's office, but also where computer operators do an employer's work at home, where not only the employee but the employee's children may be exposed to radiation. A number of studies are being done regarding possible adverse effects of sitting in front of VDTs, but as yet, there are no confirmed health hazards.[1]

From an ethical point of view, what is an employer to do? Should the employer simply take the position that because there are no studies substantially linking VDTs and birth defects, for instance, that there should be no precautions taken with regard to exposing pregnant employees to VDTs? Or, would it be preferable for an employer to allow a pregnant employee to divide her time between the VDT and other work activities during the term of her pregnancy?

What about exposing students to possible harmful effects of VDTs?

Perhaps an institution can devise options that will provide temporary diversions from unproven but possible physical dangers.

RECOMMENDATIONS

Make all reasonable efforts to inform faculty, administrators, staff, and students of institution's position regarding ethical matters.

Clarify the kind of behavior that constitutes infractions of the school or college policies and rules, and what the penalties may be.

Hold regular orientation and training sessions, especially for newcomers.

For further discussion of computer-related ethical issues see:

Hollander, P.A. (1983) University computing facilities: Some ethical dilemmas. In Baca, M.C. and Stein, R.H. (Eds.), *Ethical principles, problems, and practices in higher education.* Springfield, Ill.: C.C. Thomas Publishers.

---

[1]See e.g. The Buffalo News, June 15, 1983, at page C4 at column 1.

Appendix I

Computer Law Glossary

COMPUTER TERMS

Application Software—A specific program written to permit computer user to do his or her own job. Application software often is done by a user's in-house programmer, rather than being supplied by a seller of the system, or by an original equipment manufacturer.

Cathode Ray Tube (CRT)—A TV screen used to display information to the user.

Central Processing Unit (CPU)—This is the actual computing or calculating part of the computer. The entire computer system is usually controlled by the CPU; however, the CPU is transparent to the end-user.

Clean Power— Electric power which has been "filtered" to remove irregularities such as voltage surges and spikes as well as "noise" such as caused by electric motors, etc.

Computer—Result of the memory, input/output (I/O), and central processing unit (CPU) programmed to work together toward an end product.

Computer Assisted Design (CAD)—Consists of computer programmed graphics used in the layout, testing and design of products (usually manufacturing).

Computer Assisted Manufacturing (CAM)—Commonly referred to as robotics, today. Computers are programmed to operate specific manufacturing devices, e.g. to perform certain tasks on an assembly line for the production of automobiles, or in the production of steel.

Cursor—A white square that appears on the cathode ray tube (CRT) to show the user the next position where a character will appear on the screen.

Disk Drive— An input-output device used to store and retrieve programs and operations from inserted magnetic media.

Documentation—Instruction manuals for components of a computing system.

Floppy Disk—Small, flexible and portable, magnetic recording media used in disk drive.

Input-Output (I/O)—Input refers to keyboard, punch cards, or other device that enters data and programs into the central processing unit (CPU). Output refers to a screen , printer, tape, disk, or other device that permits the end product to be retrieved from the CPU.

Main Frame—The largest of the computers manufactured by IBM, Cyber, Cray, and others. Marked by fast CPU operating speed, almost limitless memories and storage, and a large number of users.

Main Memory—Storage place for programs and the data on which the programs operate. Usually consists of RAM Memory (Random Access Memory), supported by ROM (Read Only Memory).

Object Code—The result of compilation or translation of a higher level source code into machine readable language. Object code may be instantly run, or further compiled into machine code.

Memory Pac—Sometimes called Cachet Memory; usually, but not always, ROM (Read Only Memory). Holds specific programs used frequently in processing.

Original Equipment Manufacturer (OEM)—A company that manufactures and sells its own computer products but also buys assembled computer products designed and made by others to resell, often under its own label. An OEM takes on the mantle of the manufacturer.

Peripherals—A general term used to refer to support devices for central processing units and memories. Input-output devices would be referred to as peripherals.

Program—A series of instructions, usually used to manipulate information stored in a memory device. Programs in a computing system are referred to as software, while the electronic and mechanical parts of the system are called hardware.

Random Access Memory (RAM)—A type of memory device that can be both read and written; that is, the user can interact with the RAM.

Read Only Memory (ROM)—A program that is permanent and can be read only; that is, it cannot be changed as can a random access memory (RAM).

Reverse Engineering—The process by which a person who legitimately has acquired a product, such as computer equipment, takes it apart, learns its component parts and operation, and determines how it is designed and manufactured.

Robotics—See Computer Assisted Manufacturing. CAM's that perform tasks in a mechanical, though highly sophisticated, fashion.

The name robotics reflects the fact that many CAM's look like parts of or a complete robot, including, but not always, being able to move about and speak.

Source Code—The highest level of programs. Usually written in languages like Fortran, Basic, Cobol. A computer cannot run source code, so it must be compiled or translated into a usable form for processing. The resulting machine-usable code generally is referred to as object code.

System Software—Basic programming supplied by the manufacturer of the equipment to operate the central processing unit, the memories, and the input-output system.

Terminal—Anything to show the output of the computer; can sometimes be used for the entering of information, if so equipped.

Time-Sharing—A system by which many users may share common access to a computer.

Turnkey Systems—A computing system that is fully operational when powered-on; generally, small minis and micros.

Videotape—Defined under the Copyright Act of 1976 as the reproduction of the images and sounds of a program or programs broadcast by a television broadcast station licensed by the Federal Communications Commission; may be protected by copyright.

LEGAL TERMS

Actual Damages—Money compensation for losses resulting from breach of contract, personal injury, or property damage which readily can be shown to have been sustained and for which the injured party should be compensated as a matter of right.

Breach of Contract—A failure to perform obligations under a contract, and for which failure there is no legal excuse.

Breach of Warranty—A failure to meet the guarantee as to quality, content, condition, or title.

Collateral Estoppel—A doctrine prohibiting the relitigation of issues decided in a prior action.

Consequential Damages—Damages that were reasonably foreseeable as being probable if the contract were broken.

Contract—A set of promises; (1) made by parties competent to contract; (2) regarding a proper subject matter; (3) for proper consideration (such as money); and (4) where there is a mutuality of agreement and obligation. An oral contract is enforceable if it can be performed in less than one year.

Copyright—The protection by federal statute of the original works of authors and artists which gives them the exclusive right to publish their work or determine who may do so.

Copyright Notice—Placing appropriate information on work to inform others regarding ownership, e.g. © 1982 Jane I. Smith.

Copyright Registration—Delivery of work to the U.S. Copyright Office, along with application and fee. Registration generally is required in order for a copyright owner to file suit for infringement of the copyright.

Fair Use—A small amount of copying permitted under the federal copyright law which will not be considered an infringement of a copyright.

First Sale—The first sale doctrine is the principle that a copyright owner loses his exclusive right to sell a particular copy of his work after he parts with the title to that particular copy.

Fixed Work—Under copyright law, a work is "created" when it is "fixed" for the first time. A work is deemed to be "fixed" when it is embodied in a copy or phonorecord or videotape in sufficiently permanent form so as to be perceived or otherwise communicated, such as being reduced to writing or put on tape.

Fraud—An intentional perversion of truth for the purpose of inducing another to rely upon it to part with a valuable thing or surrender a legal right.

Independent Contractor—One who contracts to do work for another according to his own methods and is under his employer's control only as to the result.

Infringement of Copyright—A violation of the exclusive rights of a copyright owner. Remedies for infringement include: injunctions; impounding and disposition of infringing articles; damages and profits; and costs and attorney's fees.

Injunction—A court order to stop or to start a particular act, such as an injunction ordering the cessation of an infringement of copyright.

Lease—An agreement by which one relinquishes his right to immediate possession of property (e.g. a computer) while retaining title. A lease gives exclusive possession of the property against everyone including the owner. A lease must be in writing.

License—A grant of some but not all the rights embraced in a copyright. An agreement giving permission to possess property (e.g. a computer program) and use it subject to the rights of possession of the owner. A license need not be in writing.

Liquidated Damages—An amount of money set forth in a contract which the parties agree will be paid as damages owed to one party if there is a breach of contract by the other.

Negligent Misrepresentation—Negligent refers to an omission to act as a reasonable person under the circumstances. Misrepresentation refers to an untrue statement of fact.

Non-Disclosure Agreement—A promise that certain confidential information (e.g. a trade secret) will not be revealed to others as where an employee agrees not to reveal employer's confidential information, or where a prospective investor or purchaser agrees not to reveal confidential information about a new product.

Patent—Protection of an invention that excludes others from making, selling, or using it during a specified period of time.

Prima Facie Evidence—Evidence that is clear on its face at first view, needing no further explanation.

Privity of Contract—The relationship between two or more contracting parties. It is essential to the maintenance of a legal action on any contract that there be privity of contract between the plaintiff and the defendant in respect to the matter sued on. Requirement of privity is not necessary in the area of products liability.

Products Liability—A doctrine making a manufacturer strictly liable in tort when a product he places in the market, knowing it is to be used without inspection for defects, proves to have a defect that causes injury to a human being.

Proprietary Information—Information belonging to a particular owner, such as a university, a copyright owner, or a company.

Punitive Damages—Compensation in excess of actual damages, meant as a form of punishment and awarded only for willful and malicious misconduct.

Restrictive Employment Agreement—A promise by an employee in exchange for money or other value, that he will not compete with the employer for a certain period of time, in a certain geographic area, doing a certain kind of work.

Restrictive Use Covenant—A promise made as part of a contract that certain property, such as computer programs, will be limited in their use.

Severability—A breach of one clause of a contract would not necessarily mean a breach of all clauses of the contract.

Shop Rights—The right of an employer to use an employee's invention in employer's business without payment of royalties, in effect, a nonexclusive license.

Specific Performance—A requirement that a party guilty of a breach of contract perform the obligations set forth in the contract. Failure to carry out a court decree of specific performance may result in imprisonment for contempt of court.

Statutory Damages—Money compensation set forth in a statute as a remedy for violation of the statute.

Stay—A stopping of a judicial proceeding by order of a court.

Tangible Property—Property capable of being known by the senses, such as real estate or a computer program, as compared with intangible property, such as a copyright or an easement.

Tort—A civil wrong resulting from the violation of a duty. The remedy may be an injunction and/or payment of damages.

Trademark—A word or symbol protected by federal or state statute or by common law from use by others. The term *trademark* refers to a mark used to identify goods, while the term *service mark* refers to a mark used to identify services.

Trade Secret—Information protected by an equitable duty of confidentiality. To prove misappropriation of a trade secret, plaintiff must show (1) plaintiff possessed a trade secret, (2) plaintiff disclosed the trade secret to defendant, (3) plaintiff and defendant shared a confidential relationship, and (4) defendant adopted and used the secret to plaintiff's detriment.—R. Milgrim, *Trade Secrets*, Section 7.07 (1) 1983.

Unfair Competition—The practice of endeavoring to substitute one's own goods or products for those of another, having an established reputation and extensive sale, by means of imitation of name appearance—the imitation being enough to mislead the general public or deceive an unwary customer and yet not amounting to an absolute counterfeit or to the infringement of a trade mark or trade-name—*Singer Mfg. Co. v. June Mfg. Co.*, 163 U.S.169

Warranty, Full—Guaranty as to labor and materials; warrantor must remedy within reasonable time and without charge.

Warranty of Fitness For a Particular Purpose—A guaranty that goods (e.g. computer equipment) are suitable for the special purpose of the buyer, which will not be satisfied by mere fitness for general purposes.

Warranty of Merchantability—A guaranty that the goods (e.g. computer equipment) are reasonably fit for the general purposes for which they are sold.

Appendix II

Checklists

CHECKLIST—
Copyright, Patent, Trade Secret & Trademark: Some Basic Elements

	Copyright	Patent	Trade Secret	Trademark
What is protected?	Original form of expression of an idea, but not the idea itself. Computer program is copyrightable. See **Apple v. Franklin**, 714 **F**.2d 1240, 3rd Cir., 1983.	Novel, non-obvious and useful machine, process, or product. Computer program that is part of a process may be patentable. See **Diamond v. Diehr**, 450 U.S. 175, 1981.	Both Ideas and expressions; secret information that provides a competitive edge.	Distinctive word or symbol indentifying a product or commodity. (A "service mark" identifies a service.)
What law applies?	Federal: Copyright Act, 17 U.S.C. 101.	Federal: Patent Law, 35 U.S.C. 101.	State.	Usually federal: Lanham Act, 15 U.S.C. 101. State also.
When does protection begin?	Immediately upon being fixed in a tangible form.	When patent is granted.	Immediately.	Upon registration.

Duration of protection:	Life of author plus 50 years (or 75 years).	17 years.	Indefinite, until no longer secret.	20 years, plus renewals.
Form of notice:	Copyright 1984 Jane Doe (may use c in circle).	Patent Pending, or Reg. U.S. Patent Office.		R within a circle.
Cost:	Low ($10 filing fee).	High.	Cost of maintaining secrecy.	Moderate to high.
Remedies available:	Damages, Attorney's fees, Destruction of infringing copies.	Damages, Attorney's fees.	Damages, Attorney's fees.	Damages, Attorney's fees.
Further Information:	U.S. Copyright Office, Library of Congress, Washington, DC 20559 (202) 287-8700.	U.S. Patent and Trademark Office, 2021 Jefferson Davis Highway, Arlington, VA 22202 (703) 557-3158.	State.	U.S. Patent and Trademark Office, 2021 Jefferson Davis Highway, Arlington, VA 22202 (703) 557-3158.

This checklist is abbreviated in content, and is not meant to be all-inclusive; but is intended to assist readers in developing their own lists relative to their own situations.

CHECKLIST—Acquisition Contracts for Computer Systems

Yes No Action Notes

1. Is the contract written in terms of the *result* expected by the user of the system? e.g.: corporate-level recordkeeping; computer assisted manufacturing; payroll processing; registration of students.) ☐ ☐

2. Are *hardware* and *software* specified, unit by unit? ☐ ☐

3. Does the contract incorporate detailed specifications regarding computer system *performance*, such as:

   a. what specific *functions* the supplier says will be done, e.g.: providing numerical and geographical inventory data; printing tabular reports. ☐ ☐

   b. What the *supplier* will do regarding matters such as:

      1. Site preparation; ☐ ☐
      2. Date and method of delivery—penalties for delay; ☐ ☐
      3. Installation; ☐ ☐
      4. Compatibility of Components; ☐ ☐
      5. Documentation; ☐ ☐
      6. Providing personnel; ☐ ☐
      7. Training personnel; ☐ ☐
      8. Testing; ☐ ☐
      9. Guarantees of reliability; ☐ ☐
      10. Security of equipment; ☐ ☐

11. Confidentiality of user's data; ☐

12. Maintenance; ☐

13. Modifications. ☐

c. What the *user* will do regarding matters such as:

1. Providing clean power; ☐

2. Providing a proper environment; ☐

3. Providing qualified staff; ☐

4. Accepting delivery after testing. ☐

4. Financial Matters:

a. Are rental, purchase, timesharing, or service bureau terms clear, accurate, and mutually understood? ☐

b. What discounts may apply? ☐

c. What tax issues should be discussed? ☐

d. What are the penalties for partial or non-performance? ☐

e. What backups are there for downtime? ☐

5. Insurance:

a. What coverage is there for damage to, or injury resulting from, equipment or personnel? ☐

b. What coverage protects the loss of business? ☐

This checklist is abbreviated in content, and is not meant to be all-inclusive; but is intended to assist readers in developing their own lists relative to their own situations.

CHECKLIST—*Service Bureau Contracts*

	Yes	No	Action Notes
1. Does the contract between the user and the service bureau describe exactly the **services** to be performed?	☐	☐	....
e.g., conversion services, developmental services, ongoing services, input processing, report production, production of other items such as payroll checks, testing, correcting errors?	☐	☐	....
2. Is it clear what **hardware**, **software**, and **personnel** will be used to provide the services?	☐	☐	....
Will the system be available all day, every day, or when?	☐	☐	....
Is the capacity of the system able to handle user's work?	☐	☐	....
How will malfunctions be treated?	☐	☐	....
3. Are there **timetables** for all services?	☐	☐	....
Are there penalties for delays?	☐	☐	....
4. Will service bureau **duplicate user's data?**	☐	☐	....
Will bureau keep duplicates in machine code in fireproof vault off its premises?	☐	☐	....
Will user be given duplicates?	☐	☐	....
5. Are there provisions for disasters?	☐	☐	....
In case of flood, fire, etc., is there another bureau available to handle work?	☐	☐	....
Is there insurance?	☐	☐	....
6. Will the service bureau maintain **confidentiality** of user's data?	☐	☐	....
Will bureau's employees maintain confidentiality?	☐	☐	....

Is it clear that user owns its data and the medium of storage? ☐

7. What is **user** to do regarding: ☐ ☐
   Providing accurate data? ☐ ☐
   Using equipment compatible with that of service bureau? ☐ ☐

8. Is it clear how **costs** are to be calculated? ☐ ☐
   Will charges be per transaction, flat fee per month, etc? ☐ ☐
   Are there reduced fees for late services? ☐ ☐
   Is there a "most favored user" clause? ☐ ☐
   Are deadlines for payment set forth? ☐ ☐
   Is there agreement as to who pays taxes? ☐ ☐

9. Are there **warranties** by service bureau? ☐ ☐
   Does bureau represent that its system is able to perform as promised? ☐ ☐
   Will bureau indemnify user against third party claims? ☐ ☐

10. Does contract state how contract may be **terminated?** ☐ ☐

11. Does contract set out **remedies?** ☐ ☐
    Indemnification? ☐ ☐
    Penalty clauses? ☐ ☐
    Damages? ☐ ☐

12. Does contract provide for **return to user** of data? ☐ ☐
    Current source code & documentation? ☐ ☐

This checklist is abbreviated in content, and is not meant to be all-inclusive; but is intended to assist readers in developing their own lists relative to their own situations.

83

CHECKLIST—
Making Copies of Computer Programs—The Legal Perils

The creator of a computer program generally copyrights it in order to protect his or her rights to market it and gain financial benefits from it, among other things.

When another person makes a copy of a computer program that is protected with a valid copyright, without having the permission of the copyright owner, an infringement of the copyright occurs. To avoid infringing copyright, do not make copies of a copyrighted computer program without permission of the copyright owner.

The Copyright Act permits the lawful owner of a copy of a computer program to make one back-up or archival copy, and use a copy of the program in the memory of the computer during its operation. However, if the lawful owner no longer has the right to the copy, (he sells it, for example), the back-up copy must be destroyed. 17 U.S.C. section 117 (1980).

When may the lawful purchaser of a copy of a computer program lawfully make a copy?

Question	Answer
When one purchases a computer program, how many copies of it may one make?	One, to serve as a back-up.
May a purchaser make a copy to sell to a friend?	No.
May a purchaser make a copy to give to a friend?	No.
May a business purchaser make a copy to use at home?	No.

May a business purchaser make a copy to use in other computers at work?	No.
Is there any way a purchaser can make more than a back-up copy?	Of course. Get permission of the copyright owner through negotiation.
What are the possible penalties for copyright infringement?	Court order to stop copying. Destruction of copies. Damages. Costs and attorney's fees. Criminal prosecution.

NOTE: In some situations, a person who acquires a computer program may find that he or she is not, in fact, an owner of the computer program, but a licensee. For example, some software is sealed in plastic with a license inside. When the wrapping is torn open, a "tear open" or "shrink wrap" license is said to exist. A licensee is bound by the terms of the license, rather than the provisions of the Copyright Act. The license may not permit even a back-up copy.

There are legal questions about whether a person can become a licensee without knowing about that possibility until opening the package. The legal community cannot speak with assurance about the validity of shrink-wrap licenses until the courts have ruled on the matter. Meantime, many lawyers tend to view that making a back-up copy under such circumstances probably is reasonable, and certainly is prudent. At least one state, Louisiana, is said to be legislating on the validity of shrink-wrap licenses.

This checklist is abbreviated in content, and is not meant to be all-inclusive; but is intended to assist readers in developing their own lists relative to their own situations.

CHECKLIST—
"Fair Use" of Computer Programs by Teachers, Scholars, and Researchers

☐ **What is "fair use?"**

Answer: "Fair use" is a legal doctrine that permits copying of computer programs for purposes of teaching, scholarship, and research that otherwise would be deemed an infringement of copyright. The Copyright Act provides that:

"... the fair use of a copyrighted work, ... for purposes such as criticism, comment, news reporting, teaching (including multiple copies for classroom use), scholarship, or research, is not an infringement of copyright." 17 U.S.C. sec. 107 (1976).

☐ **How does one determine whether any particular use is a "fair use?"**

Answer: The Copyright Act provides that in determining whether the use made of a work in any particular case is a fair use the factors to be considered shall include:

(1) "The purpose and character of the use, including whether such use is of a commercial nature or is for nonprofit educational purposes;"

(2) "the nature of the copyrighted work;"

(3) "the amount and substantiality of the portion used in relation to the copyrighted work as a whole;" and,

☐ **Does fair use permit copying programs from floppy disks to hard disks?**

Answer: Yes, if the floppy disk is owned and the copy is created as an essential step in utilizing the machine, and for no other purpose.

☐ **Does fair use permit lending a purchased program to students in a serial fashion?**

Answer: Yes, just as one would lend a library book to students in serial fashion.

However, it is not permissible to permit all students to have copies made from the one lawful copy, just as it would not be permissible to make enough copies of a library book so that all students could have copies simultaneously.

☐ **Is it fair use to purchase twenty copies of a program for use by students in one class, and then use the same twenty copies for a subsequent class?**

Answer: Yes. One may purchase and own multiple copies of a computer program and lend them for short periods of time, just as one would do with textbooks. Be sure a back-up copy is made for each purchased copy in case copies lent out are destroyed.

(4) "the effect of the use upon the potential market for or value of the copyrighted work." 17 U.S.C. sec. 107 (1976)

☐ **Does "fair use" permit copying a whole computer program?**

Answer: No, anymore than fair use would permit copying a whole book. (Remember, however, that Sec. 117 of the Copyright Act does permit making one copy or adaptation to be used in the functioning of the machine, i.e. in the memory of the machine, and also permits making one backup copy.)

☐ **Does fair use permit teachers to print the program code to illustrate points in programming classes or prepare derivative works for the same purposes?**

Answer: Probably yes.

☐ **Does fair use permit buying one copy of a computer program and then making twenty more, one for each student's machine?**

Answer: No.

☐ **Suppose students make personal copies from programs lawfully lent to them. Are we liable to the copyright owner for aiding and abetting infringement of copyright?**

Answer: Taking reasonable precautions in the classroom and elsewhere to attempt to prevent unauthorized copying should help counter infringement charges.

☐ **Is there a way to acquire multiple copies of software other than by purchasing them piecemeal?**

Answer: Yes, try to negotiate bulk purchases or persuade software companies to make a tax-favored donation.

☐ **Does the doctrine of fair use apply to software acquired under a license, rather than by a sale?**

Answer: No. The terms of the license control what copies may be made, rather than the terms of the copyright law. Consider negotiating a site license, or try to persuade licensors to donate permission to use the software.

For further discussion of fair use, see Brooks, D.T. (1985) Fair Use of Computer Software by Educators. *EDUCOM Bulletin,* Summer 1985, Vol. 20 No. 2.

This checklist is abbreviated in content, and is not meant to be all-inclusive; but is intended to assist readers in developing their own lists relative to their own situations.

CHECKLIST—
Licensing Computer Software

Are you a developer of computer programs, but do not want to use or sell them yourself? You may wish to grant a license to someone else to use or sell the programs you develop in return for a royalty fee.

Do you want to use or sell computer programs, but do not want to develop them yourself? You may wish to pay a royalty fee to secure a license to use or sell programs developed by someone else.

Here are some basic issues to be considered when negotiating a computer software license:

Action Notes

1. What is the **subject matter** of the license?

  • Be specific in defining what is being licensed. Is the license only for the program, or does it include other items such as the object code, system flow charts, operator instructions, and user manuals?

....

2. What **use** of the licensed material is permitted?

  • Is the use restricted to a specific machine? To a specific room? To a specific building? Is there a set fee for use beyond that stated, or must additional use be negotiated?

....

3. Are there different royalty arrangements available for different **categories of users**

  • What arrangements are there, for example, for use "in-house" by data processing service providers as compared to licensors who are selling software to others? Such provisions often are referred to as "field-of-user" limitations.

....

4. What **royalties** will be paid?

  • Is a percentage royalty to be paid on each program? Is there a minimum royalty? What about an advance? When are royalties to be paid? Are royalties due on items other than the program? Are any items free?

....

5. May **copies** be made?
   - What copies are permissible under the license, in addition to back-up copies? Who owns the copies? . . . .

6. May **modifications** be made?
   - If so, what provisions are made for removal of the licensed material from the enhanced work, at the time of termination of the license? . . . .

7. What provisions are there for maintaining **confidentiality** of the licensed material?
   - Who had access to the licensed material during the term of the license? . . . .

8. What promises are made regarding date of **delivery**?
   - Is there a penalty for delays? . . . .

9. What constitutes **acceptance** of the specified material?
   - Is the material being delivered all at once, or piecemeal? Is it being tested as it is being installed? What is the meaning of being "operational?" . . . .

10. What **warranty** is provided?
    - What liability does the licensor accept, if any, regarding consequential damages? . . . .

11. What if the licensor goes bankrupt?
    - Has provision been made to place the source code in escrow and keep it updated? . . . .

12. When and how does the license **terminate?**
    - What materials are to be returned to the licensor? . . . .

This checklist is abbreviated in content, and is not meant to be all-inclusive; but is intended to assist readers in developing their own lists relative to their own situations.

89

CHECKLIST—
Employment Contracts re Intellectual Property Rights

	Yes	No	Action Notes

1. Is there an appropriate set of employment documents, e.g.
   —general employee manual?
   —individualized employee contracts?
   —separate non-employee contracts (for consultants, etc.)?

2. Does the general employee manual, or other document, set forth:

   a. The employer's general policies regarding intellectual property rights?

   b. Are copyrights, patents, and trade secrets treated consistently?

   c. A list of employer's proprietary property—such as copyrights, patents, and trade secrets—that are to be kept confidential and/or are owned by employer?

   d. A reference to professional standards or ethics to be followed by professional employees?

3. Do employee contracts for higher level employees, whose work products are more likely to be deemed work made for hire, contain:

   a. A clear job description, including present and contemplated tasks, so as to avoid questions of "lack of new consideration?"

   b. A statement of present ownership of intellectual property, such as, that all works are the property of the employer, or that the employer has a right of first refusal?

c. A provision that all works are to be disclosed to the employer, regardless of ownership? ☐ ☐ ....

d. A non-competition agreement, reasonable as to work, time, and geographic area? ☐ ☐ ....

4. Do employee contracts for lower level employees, whose work products are less likely to be deemed work made for hire, contain:

a. An accurate job description? ☐ ☐ ....

b. An indication of which ideas and works are property of employer? ☐☐☐ ☐☐☐ ....

c. A provision for transfer of ownership for compensation? ☐ ☐ ....

d. A disclosure provision? ☐ ☐ ....

5. Do non-employee contracts (e.g. with consultants) contain:

a. A clear definition of the project or task? ☐ ☐ ....

b. A statement that the work product is, or is not, to be considered a work made for hire owned by employer? ☐ ☐ ....

c. If not a work made for hire, has the consultant agreed to sell the copyright or only the copy? ☐☐☐ ☐☐☐ ....

d. Are patent and trade secrets treated consistently? ☐ ☐ ....

e. Is disclosure required? ☐ ☐ ....

f. Will ownership be conveyed to employer pending arbitration of scope of employment or reasonableness of royalty if not a work for hire? ☐☐ ☐☐ ....

g. Does employer have a right of first refusal? ☐ ☐ ....

h. If author exercised statutory right to reevaluation, how is risk of error in original valuation handled? ☐ ☐ ....

This checklist is abbreviated in content, and is not meant to be all-inclusive; but is intended to assist readers in developing their own lists relative to their own situations.

CHECKLIST—Computer Crime Statutes
Information Current as of September, 1984

STATE and STATUTE	CRIME	AMOUNT OF DAMAGE	PENALTY			
			Imprisonment Min.	Max.	Fine Min.	Max.
ALASKA* §11.46.985	Deceiving a machine (Applies to offenses that require deception as an element, as in theft by deception.)	Less than $50		90 days		$1,000
		$50 - $500		1 year		$5,000
		$500 - $25,000		5 years		$50,000
		More than $25,000		10 years		$50,000
ARIZONA*	Computer fraud, 1st degree (with intent to deceive)			5 years		$150,000
§13-2316	Computer fraud, 2nd degree (Unauthorized access, damage or destruction)			1½ years		$150,000
CALIFORNIA §502	Computer fraud Altering computerized credit information Computer damage or destruction		*All offenses* 1 year	3 years		$10,000
COLORADO* §18-5.5-102	Computer fraud Computer damage or destruction	Less than $50		6 mos.		
		$50 - $200	3 mos.	1 year	$50	$750
		$200 - $10,000	2 years	4 years	$250	$1,000
		More than $10,000	4 years	8 years		
DELAWARE §858	Computer fraud Computer damage or destruction		2 years	20 years	Individuals; Ct.'s discretion.	
				7 years	Corporations; up to $10,000.	

State / Statute	Offense	Value	Sentence	Fine
FLORIDA*				
§815.04	Offenses against intellectual property			
	With intent to defraud		5 years	$5,000
			15 years	$15,000
§815.05	Offenses against computer equipment			
	With intent to defraud		1 year	$1,000
			5 years	$5,000
	Computer damage or destruction	Less than $200	1 year	$1,000
		$200 - $1,000	5 years	$5,000
		More than $1,000, or causes interruption of gov't or public facility.	15 years	$15,000
§815.06	Offenses against computer users			
	With intent to defraud		5 years	$5,000
			15 years	$15,000
GEORGIA*				
§16-9-93	Computer fraud		15 years	2½ x the amount of theft
	Computer damage or destruction		15 years	$50,000
ILLINOIS				
ch. 38 §16.9	Unauthorized use of computer			$500
	Modification or destruction of programs or data	Less than $1,000		$500
		More than $1,000		$1,000
	Computer fraud	Less than $1,000	1 year	$1,000
		More than $1,000	3 years	Amount of loss or $10,000
MICHIGAN			*All offenses*	
§752.794	Computer fraud	Less than $100	90 days	$100
		More than $100	10 years	$5,000

(cont. next page)

STATE and STATUTE	CRIME	AMOUNT OF DAMAGE	PENALTY Imprisonment Min.	Max.	Fine Min.	Max.
MICHIGAN				*All offenses*		
§752.795	Computer damage or destruction					
§752.796	Use of computer to commit: embezzlement; fraudulent disposition of personal property; larceny; larceny by conversion	Less than $100 More than $100		90 days 10 years		$100 $5,000
MINNESOTA						
§609.88	Computer damage or destruction Alteration of computer with intent to defraud	Less than $500 $500 - $2,500 More than $2,500		90 days 5 years 10 years		$500 $5,000 $50,000
§609.89	Use of computer in theft Theft of computer	Less than $500 $500 - $2,500 More than $2,500		90 days 5 years 10 years		$500 $5,000 $50,000
MISSOURI						
§569.095	Tampering with intellectual property Modification or destruction of computer data Disclosure or theft—trade secrets With intent to defraud	More than $150		1 year 5 years		$1,000 2 x gain to $20,000
§569.097	Tampering with computer equipment With intent to defraud	Less than $150 More than $150 More than $1,000, or causes interruption of gov't or public facility		1 year 5 years 7 years		$1,000 2 x gain to $20,000 2 x gain to $20,000

	Offense	Value	Term	Fine
§569.099	Tampering with computer users (unauthorized access, denial of computer services.) With intent to defraud	More than $150	1 year 5 years	$1,000 2 x gain to $20,000
MONTANA §45-6-311	Unlawful use of computer (unauthorized use, altering or destroying programs, computer fraud).	Up to $300 More than $300	6 mos. 10 years	$500 2 x loss to victim
NEW MEXICO §30-16-3	Use of computer to defraud Use of computer for embezzlement or theft	Less than $100 $100 - $2,500 More than $2,500	18 mos. 6 mos. 18 mos. 3 years	$5,000 $500 $5,000 $5,000
§30-16-4	Unauthorized computer use	Less than $100 $100 - $2,500 More than $2,500	6 mos. 18 mos. 3 years	$500 $5,000 $5,000
NEW YORK (Proposed)	Computer trespass Computer tampering		1 year 4 years	_All offenses_ $5,000 or double the profit of computer crime
NORTH CAROLINA				
§14-454	Computer fraud		10 years	Discretionary
§14-455	Damaging computers and related materials		10 years	Discretionary
§14-456	Denial of computer services to authorized user		2 years	Discretionary
§14-457	Extortion via threats to damage computer		10 years	Discretionary

STATE and STATUTE	CRIME	AMOUNT OF DAMAGE	Imprisonment Min.	Imprisonment Max.	Fine Min.	Fine Max.
OHIO						
§2901.01	Expansion of definitions section to include computer-related terms.					
RHODE ISLAND			*All offenses:*			
§11-52-2	Computer fraud					
§11-52-3	Computer damage or destruction	More than $500		5 years		$5,000
§11-52-4	Theft of computer-related materials					
UTAH*			*All Offenses:*			
§76-6-703	Computer fraud	Less than $25		90 days		$299
	Computer damage or destruction	$25 - $100		6 mos.		$1,000
		$100 - $300		1 year		$5,000
		$300 - $1,000		5 years		$10,000
		More than $1,000		15 years		
VIRGINIA						
§18.2-152.3	Computer fraud (including embezzlement and larceny)	Less than $200		1 year		$1,000
		More than $200	1 year	10 years	or 1 year /	$1,000
§18.2-152.4	Computer trespass: Removing data; causing malfunction; alter, create or erase data; injure property.			1 year		$1,000
§18.2-152.5	Computer invasion of privacy: (Unauthorized examination of personal or financial data)					$500
§18.2-152.6	Theft of computer services			1 year		$1,000

		Sentence		Fine
§18.2-152.7	Personal trespass by computer, cause physical injury:	5 years	20 years	
	If malicious			
	If non-malicious		1 year	$1,000
WISCONSIN				
§943.70	Offenses against computer data and programs			
	With intent to defraud		9 mos.	$10,000
	More than $2,500, or causes interruption of gov't or public facility.		2 years	$10,000
			5 years	$10,000
	Offenses against computer equipment and supplies			
	With intent to defraud		9 mos.	$10,000
	More than $2,500, or causes interruption of gov't or public facility.		2 years	$10,000
			5 years	$10,000

*Alaska: Organizations may be fined the greater of $100,000 or 3 times the gain resulting from the offense.

*Arizona: Sentences of imprisonment may be increased 25% or decreased 50%, depending on circumstances. Organizations may be fined up to $1,000,000.

*Colorado: Depending on the value of the property involved, corporations could be fined either $1,000 - $30,000 or $5,000 - $50,000.

*Florida: Fines may be increased up to two times the gain resulting from the offense or loss suffered by the victim.

*Georgia: §16-9-95 offers immunity from civil liability to those who report violations of computer crime laws in good faith.

*Utah: Depending on the value of the property involved, corporations could be fined from $300 to $10,000.

This checklist is abbreviated in content, and is not meant to be all-inclusive; but is intended to assist readers in developing their own lists relative to their own situations.

CHECKLIST—*Insurance for Computers*

I.COMPUTERS, PROGRAMS AND DATA INSURANCE

Property insurance is available to cover computers, programs, and data. Before selecting a policy, take into account the following issues:

A.Business Computers

1. If your general "all risks" business insurance policy does not protect satisfactorily against accidental damage to computers, ask about special computer insurance policies that are available for computers, terminals, peripherals, programs, data, storage media.

2. Computers are especially vulnerable to damage by moisture, heat, and electrical problems such as surges of power and static electricity, seek the broadest possible coverage, such as protection against:

☐ water   ☐ malfunction of
☐ storm damage   other equipment
☐ floods   ☐ vandalism
☐ fire   ☐ malicious damage
☐ explosion   ☐ theft
☐ earthquakes   ☐ erasure of data by
☐ electrical failure   magnet or electricity

3. Does the insurance pay replacement value or depreciated value?

4. Regarding software programs and data, will the insurance pay only to replace blank disks, or will it pay the cost of reentering and or reconstructing the data on the disks?

5. What coverage is available for computers while in transit from one site to another?

V.SOURCES OF COMPUTER INSURANCE COVERAGE:*

Many insurance companies offer protection for computers and computer-related activities. The following list is not meant to be all-inclusive.

Fireman's Fund   Ohio Casualty
Hanover   Safeco
Hartford   Unigard
Kemper   United Pacific Reliance

VI.SPECIALIZED COMPUTER INSURANCE POLICIES:

(Partial listing, data subject to change.)

A.**AppleCare**, applications available from authorized Apple dealers.

Apple Computer has fostered AppleCare, a special "all-risk" policy underwritten by the Chubb Group and available through Emett & Chandler, Inc. AppleCare is said to cover one's Apple system, i.e., hardware, software, and accessories, anywhere in the world. AppleCare reportedly covers earthquakes, floods, and electrical and mechanical breakdown, but not programming error or data erasure by magnet or electricity.

Deductible: $100.

Cost: $25 protects system valued to $5000.
$50 to protect up to $25,000.

After premium is paid, any additional equipment bought is covered automatically up to the $25,000 limit at no additional cost.

B.**Safeware.** 2929 North High St., Columbus, OH 43202, (800) 848-3469 or (614) 262-0559.

Standard policy does not cover cost of replacing data, but special policy, "Big Mike" will, up to $5000.

Deductible: $50

Cost: $35 minimum premium, and $15 increments per $3000 of coverage.

Discounts: for university students at schools requiring use of, and/or having large volume of computer sales to students.

C. **The Personal Computer Insurance Agency,** P.O. Box 28506, San Jose, CA 95159, (408) 723-8107

Coverage includes damage due to corrosion or air conditioning.

Deductible: None

Cost: Slightly higher premium.

Extra: $10 per month provides "business interruption" option paying up to $2500 per month if down at crucial moment.

D. **Data Security Insurance Agency,** 4800 Riverbend Rd., Boulder, CO 80301, (303) 443-3600 (contact company for details).

Note:

In addition to acquiring insurance, remember to make hard copies of all data, and consider getting surge protectors.

B. Home Computers

1. If computer is used only at home for games & hobbies, not for business purposes at home, will homeowner/renter policy provide protection?
2. What additional premium will be required?
3. If a computer is used at home for business purposes, will it be defined as a "business machine," for which the insurance company will pay only depreciated value, not replacement value?
4. How can one assure that replacement value will be paid?

II. LOSS OF BUSINESS

Does your policy cover loss of business due to interruptions or downtime?

III. PROGRAMMING ERRORS

Consider personal liability insurance to protect programmers or data base owners from claims of material loss resulting from:

☐ errors in a program, ☐ omission of data from program, data base.

IV. INJURY TO PERSONS

Review accident insurance regarding coverage for personal injuries or death caused by:

☐ electrical shock   ☐ leaking radiation
☐ noxious fumes   ☐ malfunctioning robotic arm

*Examples of specific insurance companies and policies from: V. Schatmeier. "Insurance—Protecting Your Computer Investment." In: A+ Magazine, November, 1984, p.79.

Appendix III

Copyright Law Amended Regarding Computer Programs

The following excerpt amending title 17, United States Code, is taken from Public Law 96-517, dated December 12, 1980 (94 STAT. 3028-29).

Sec. 10. (a) Section 101 of title 17 of the United States Code is amended to add at the end thereof the following new language:

"A 'computer program' is a set of statements or instructions to be used directly or indirectly in a computer in order to bring about a certain result.".

(b) Section 117 of title 17 of the United States Code is amended to read as follows:

"§ 117.[1] Limitations on exclusive rights: Computer programs

"Notwithstanding the provisions of section 106,[2] it is not an infringement for the owner of a copy of a computer program to make or authorize the making of another copy or adaptation of that computer program provided:

"(1) that such a new copy or adaptation is created as an essential step in the utilization of the computer program in conjunction with a machine and that it is used in no other manner, or

"(2) that such new copy or adaptation is for archival purposes only and that all archival copies are destroyed in the event that continued possession of the computer program should cease to be rightful.

"Any exact copies prepared in accordance with the provisions of this section may be leased, sold, or otherwise transferred, along with the copy from which such copies were prepared, only as part of the lease, sale, or other transfer of all rights in the program. Adaptations so prepared may be transferred only with the authorization of the copyright owner.".

---

[1] 17 USC 117.
[2] 17 USC 106.

Appendix IV

Resources for Legal Information in Secondary and Higher Education

If you have found the information contained in this monograph to be helpful in your day-to-day operations and as a reference it is quite likely that you may also be interested in other titles included in the *The Higher Education Administration Series* or in our publications that offer quarterly updates on case law related to various fields of education.

Following is a list of titles available from College Administration Publications. Where the titles are not illustrative of the subject covered, a brief description is included. If you wish to order, there is an order blank on the reverse side of this sheet which you may wish to copy rather than tearing out this page.

Other titles in *The Higher Education Administration Series:*
- ► Administering College and University Housing:
  A Legal Perspective
- ► The Dismissal of Students with Mental Disorders:
  Legal Issues, Policy Considerations
  and Alternative Responses
- ► Computers in Education:
  Legal Liabilities and Ethical Issues
  Concerning Their Use and Misuse

The following publications offer the reader a quarterly report on recent precedent setting higher court decisions covering a wide range of subjects in the area encompassed by the self-descriptive title. In addition, through the accumulated back issues, and in the "College" publications, a casebook, each of these publications are also excellent comprehensive references that can be of great help in day-to-day operations and long range planning:
- ► The College Student and the Courts
- ► The College Administrator and the Courts
- ► The Schools and the Courts

While primarily written for practicing administrators, superintendents, school boards, teachers and legal counsel in secondary education, this publication is of great value to related schools of education.

Order Blank

Bill to:............................ Ship to:............................

....

....

Quantity	Item & Price	Total
_____	**The Dismissal of Students with Mental Disorders:** 1 to 9 copies @ $9.95; 10 or more copies @ $9.50	_____
_____	**Administering College and University Housing:** 1 to 9 copies @ $9.95; 10 or more copies @ $9.50	_____
_____	**A Practical Guide to Legal Issues Affecting** **College Teachers** 1 to 9 copies @ $4.95; 10 to 24 copies @ $3.95; 25 or more copies @ $3.50	_____
_____	**Computers in Education:** **Legal Liabilities and Ethical Issues** **Concerning Their Use and Misuse** 1 to 9 copies @ $9.95; 10 or more copies @ $9.50	_____
_____	**The College Student and the Courts** Includes casebook, all back issues and four quarterly updating supplements.............$98.50	_____
_____	**The College Administrator and the Courts** Includes casebook, all back issues and four quarterly updating supplements.............$77.50	_____
_____	**The Schools and the Courts** Includes over 600 pages of back issues and four updating reports.........................$67.50	_____

Postage (if payment accompanies order we will ship postpaid) _____

North Carolina residents add appropriate sales tax _____

Total _____

Address Orders to:
College Administration Publications, Inc.
Dept. CM, P.O. Box 8492, Asheville, NC 28814

☐ Pricing of the above publications was correct on the publication date of this monograph. If you wish to be advised of current prices of titles you have ordered before shipment, please check.

☐ For further information regarding any of the above titles please indicate with check here and in the quantity column of each publication and we will forward current brochures and information.

PRAISE FOR *THE SACRED MEAL*

"This is the book I have been waiting for—to give to seekers who are wary of pious language, to believers who have dozed off in their pews, to pastors who want to know how to speak in fresh ways of old truths, to anyone who asks me why I am still Christian. This is the book I have been waiting to give, but it is also the book I have been waiting to read. In it, Nora Gallagher does just what holy communion does: she folds sacred life and ordinary life together like a sandwich, holding it out to me so that I suddenly remember how hungry I am. There is not a trite or phony word in this book. It is full of real people, real life, real food—and above all a real Jesus, who keeps dying and rising into this world God so loves."

Barbara Brown Taylor, author of
Leaving Church and *Feasting on the Word*

"It's so fitting that Nora Gallagher would write on the sacramental meal, because that's how I've always felt about her writing . . . it opens up a channel of grace and offers a taste of mystery, accessible to anyone, yet so full of meaning that the inside feels bigger than the outside. *The Sacred Meal* is a rich meal for the soul, and will be a great book to share among a circle of friends too."

Brian McLaren, author/activist
(brianmclaren.net)

"Nora Gallagher is a writer I would follow anywhere, but it is a particular thrill to follow her to the Lord's Table; I know of no contemporary writer whose insights about the Eucharist match hers."

Lauren F. Winner, Duke Divinity School,
author of *Girl Meets God*

"Eucharist. Communion. The Lord's Supper. We Christians can't even agree what to call this most holy and most contentious element of our faith. What Nora Gallagher has succeeded in doing, however, is to craft a text that can bring us together so that Jesus' prayer that we 'may all be one' might be imagined. For if that's going to happen, it's going to happen around the Lord's Table, sharing a sacred meal."

Tony Jones, author of *The New Christians*
(tonyj.net)

THE SACRED MEAL

THE SACRED MEAL

nora gallagher

THOMAS NELSON
Since 1798

NASHVILLE   DALLAS   MEXICO CITY   RIO DE JANEIRO   BEIJING

Published in Nashville, Tennessee, by Thomas Nelson. Thomas Nelson is a registered trademark of Thomas Nelson, Inc.

Thomas Nelson, Inc., titles may be purchased in bulk for educational, business, fund-raising, or sales promotional use. For information, please e-mail SpecialMarkets@ThomasNelson.com.

Unless otherwise noted, Scripture quotations are taken from the NEW REVISED STANDARD VERSION of the Bible. © 1989 by the Division of Christian Education of the National Council of the Churches of Christ in the U.S.A. All rights reserved.

Scripture quotations marked NLT are from the *Holy Bible*, New Living Translation. © 1996, 2004. Used by permission of Tyndale House Publishers, Inc., Carol Stream, Illinois 60188. All rights reserved.

Library of Congress Cataloging-in-Publication Data
Gallagher, Nora, 1949–
  The sacred meal / Nora Gallagher.
     p. cm.
  Includes bibliographical references.
  ISBN 978-0-8499-0092-1 (hardcover)
  1. Lord's Supper. I. Title.
  BV825.3.G36 2009
  234'.163--dc22

                                   2009024633

Printed in the United States of America
09 10 11 12 13 WCF 9 8 7 6 5 4 3 2

For Lucy

CONTENTS

ACKNOWLEDGMENTS

My thanks to Flip Brophy, Elizabeth Garnsey, Cynthia Gorney, Jodie Ireland, Ann Jaqua, and Barbara Brown Taylor.

FOREWORD

Over the centuries, one of the two or three major unifying elements of the Christian experience has been the observance, by reenactment, of the last meal that Jesus and His disciples ate together in the Upper Room before His arrest in the Garden of Gethsemane. Sometimes known today as the Lord's Supper, sometimes as the Eucharist, sometimes as the mass, and sometimes just simply as holy communion, that sacred meal has been referred to over the years of Christian history by many names. But regardless of which name has been assigned to it at any given time in any given place by any given group of believers, the sacred meal has remained as a thread common to all the disparate groups within the larger Christian family, for it is the one that most keenly marks Christian as Christian and community as community.

There have also been doctrinal differences, of course, about the exact nature and proper understanding of what transpires in the taking of the communion food and drink. Some might even say that many of those differences have been dogmatic ones, while still others can persuasively argue that the resulting quarrels have been as superficial as they have been painful. But the questions about whether the bread of communion is the body of Jesus transubstantiated or whether it serves symbolically as that body or whether it functions only as a remembrance, ultimately make no difference in one central fact: when Christians participate in the sacrament of the shared table, they are remembering that pivotal night and those compelling words that still ring down over the millennia: "This bread is My flesh, broken for you, and this cup is My blood, shed for you. Do this in remembrance of Me."

So we eat, and we remember . . . and may God forbid that ever there should be a time when some of us do not weep as we share that common table, just as, pray God, no single one of us should ever join our fellows around that table without being, from time to time, among the ones who weep. Communion is where we join, one with another in God, as in no other act and no other practice within this life; and the joining is exquisite in its joy and its sorrow, its nurture and its costs.

Because the sacred meal is so holy and so central, thousands of words have been expended on it. Undoubtedly other thousands will likewise be devoted to it in the future. Those words and the books and essays constructed from them have added, and will continue to add, greatly to the Church's understanding of the history of the Lord's Supper, of the doctrines that have swirled around it, of the various liturgies that inform it, of a myriad of circumstances that may attend it. But this book about communion is not principally about any of those things. Rather, this book is about one Christian's lifelong engagement with the Eucharist and about the richness of being sometimes among the weeping, and sometimes among the serving, and sometimes among the rejoicing. This is, in sum, a deeply personal and deeply confessional book, written by a singularly gifted and skilled writer, about the Eucharist . . . about that practice which is central to her faith.

This book also, and obviously, belongs to a series of books. That is, it is one in a set of eight books. Seven of those volumes treat the seven ancient practices that inform Christianity, and the eighth volume, which in actuality is the first of them, is an introduction not only to the practices themselves and what they are, but also to the concept of practices and their role in the formation of the Christian life. Every one of those ancient practices—fixed-hour prayer, Sabbath observance, the keeping of the liturgical year, pilgrimage, tithing, fasting, and the sacred meal—has been in and with Christianity from the beginning, but none of them has the poetry, the stark, steely anamnesis of the sacred meal. And no presentation of the sacred meal and its terrible power to make of us one body in Christ, will ever be more simply, more directly, or more compellingly written than is this one by Nora Gallagher.

Amen.

Phyllis Tickle
General Editor
Ancient Practices Series

INTRODUCTION

WHEN THE EDITORS OF THIS SERIES CALLED TO SAY THEY were working on books about ancient practices, I was ready with my answer: no. I was sitting in an airport parking lot on my cell phone. My hand was actually on my car keys. And then they said the words *Holy Communion*. I must have said something like, "Huh," and I put the keys down. Because (a) I had never thought about Communion as a practice, (b) it's the one practice I've stuck with, and (c) I had thought about Communion from two perspectives, that of layperson and as a prospective Episcopal priest. (I went through the entire "process" of seeking ordination and, having been invited by the church to go forward, changed my mind. I wrote about this in my memoir, *Practicing Resurrection*.)

While there may be many persons more qualified than I am to write such a book (and you will be the judge of that), I am uniquely qualified in this regard: I have served the bread at Communion, a job almost always reserved for a priest (in every interview with ministry commissions, it is wise, those who have been through the process of seeking Episcopal ordination know, to mention your special affection for Communion). I have also served the wine, and I have been on the receiving end more times than I can count. Every time it is the same, and every time it is different.

I sat there in my car in the parking lot with jet engines winding up and shutting down on the runway thirty feet away, and thought about the many times I had participated in this most ancient of Christian practices, this odd, mysterious, ritualized eating and drinking that has been part of the fabric of this faith in all probability since its inception. I thought about the first time I saw people at Communion, when I was eight in a Roman Catholic church in New Mexico with my best friend at that age; then I thought about the last time I had taken Communion, which was on the trip I had just returned from, in the light-filled sanctuary of Grace Church, Bainbridge Island, with my first cousin.

As I sat there remembering various Communions, in various churches or out in fields or at funerals or weddings, in big cities and in small towns, I realized that I was also remembering many of the people who had stood or knelt near or next to me, even if I did not know their names. In most instances it was a roll of the dice who would be there, who would end up huffing to his knees next to me on some cushion at the altar rail or standing upright in a circle, what child might settle herself so close by that our knees nearly touched, or what woman's skirt might brush mine.

There we were, my memory said. *You were with them and they were with you. For a moment, you were part of a great web of strangers, drawn on that day to that one place, traveling toward something invisible, just around the corner, something that made us all drop everything else to be there.*

To engage in a practice is to show up and not get attached to the outcome. Unlike a habit, like driving down the same street from work to home every day, the purpose of a spiritual practice is to help us stay awake. Hidden in this kind of repetition is the chance that on any given day, the mind or the soul will connect with what is waiting to connect to us.

At the heart of any religion worth its salt, I think, is what a friend calls "redemptive wrestling." Faith is all about struggle. It's about getting to what is really *real* in a world that does not always welcome reality.

We think of doubt as the enemy of faith, but I am more inclined to think that self-satisfaction and illusion are faith's foes. "Faith without doubt," a friend said, "even desperate doubt, is flat faith indeed." Doubt is our good cop: it keeps faith honest. Real faith is energetic. It is centered and released in redemptive wrestling.

A spiritual practice is a place where the heart and mind and soul are trained in wrestling, not with doubt but with illusion. What is life-giving is often hidden. We live in a world where we mistake riches for sustenance, a new purse (or you fill in the blank) for food, power over others for agency or our own empowerment. It is often harder to do good than it is to do evil. We need all the help we can get. Think of a spiritual practice as Pilates for the spirit.

I don't come by these words easily. I am very good at starting things out and very thin on maintenance. Get me involved in a project in its early stages, and I am your woman. I'll roll up my sleeves and jump into any new enterprise, dream big dreams, and come up with solutions for everything. ("Please," my husband said to me last week after I decried the subway schedule in the Big Apple, "do not try to reform the city of New York.") But a few months or a year down the road, I start to wander, my eyes on a new enterprise. I take to a new practice like a duck to water: Walking the labyrinth, oh yes! Meditation, just try me! How about centering prayer? You bet. But in truth, I have dropped them all over the years, usually before they could have any real effect. So for me to write about practice is a little like asking Oprah to talk about diets. She's tried a lot of them but stuck with few, and I know that state well. If you could nail me with any practice, you could say I practice avoidance.

About three minutes after I agreed to write this book, I panicked. I was not a worthy guide. But before I called back and reneged, I thought about how much this practice meant to me. There have been weeks when I went to every Eucharist I could find. A Communion glutton. Maybe writing about the practice of Communion would help me understand why it held so much meaning for me, just as writing about silence helped Thomas Merton, the Trappist monk and author, as his editor Patrick Hart put it, to become silent.

You will find in these pages a way to approach communion by a threefold path: waiting, receiving, and afterward. A (mercifully) brief history of Communion, and various Christian perspectives on it. Mostly, you find my story, which is the only story I can truthfully tell. My practice of taking Communion goes on; sometimes it is for me a perfectly ordinary event; sometimes it's as if the floor dropped out from underneath my feet. I show up, again and again, a miracle in itself.

1

SCOTCH TAPE AND BALING WIRE

*The ultimate source of the Susquehanna River was a kind of meadow in
which nothing happened: no cattle, no mysteriously gushing water, merely
the slow accumulation of moisture from many unseen and unimportant
sources, the gathering of dew, so to speak, the beginning, the unspectacular
congregation of nothingness, the origin of purpose. And where the moisture
stood, sharp rays of bright sunlight were reflected back until the whole
area seemed golden, and hallowed, as if here life itself were beginning.
This is how everything begins—the mountains, the oceans, life itself. A
slow accumulation—the gathering together of meaning.*

—JAMES A. MICHENER, CHESAPEAKE

WHEN MY HUSBAND AND I WALKED INTO THE BAKERY, I
knew something was wrong. My friend Jodie was pushing back
tears with the heel of her hand. Frank, her husband, was sitting across the table from her, somber, watchful. *Are they getting a
divorce?* I thought. *Has something happened to one of the children?* I put
my hand on Jodie's shoulder and sat down.

"What's wrong?"

"It's Frankie," Jodie said. "Val's daughter. You remember Val and Kirk?"

"Yes, I do." Val, an architect, a woman whose face was all kindness. Kirk, her husband, handsome, gentle, a builder. Francesca, Frankie, their younger daughter. How old was she now? Twelve? I remembered Frankie and her sister, sweet little girls in dresses, at a party years ago, too shy to talk to strangers, and Val leaning down to talk to the littler one like a mother hen covering her daughter with a wing.

"She's missing in Panama. A small plane."

The call had come the night before, Sunday.

Frankie was on vacation with a school friend, Thalia Klein, and Thalia's father, Michael Klein. Michael, age thirty-seven, had taken the two girls in a chartered Cessna that day from Islas Secas off Panama's Pacific coast, heading for the Chiriqui volcano, about 285 miles west of the capital. In rain and fog, the pilot of the plane had radioed the airport at a town named David that he could not see the runway to land and had then disappeared. Witnesses said later that they saw or heard a small plane flying too low in the jungle toward the mountains.

As soon as they got the call, Val and Kirk had asked a neighbor to drive them to the airport in Los Angeles. Kim Klein, Thalia's mother, and Robert Klein, Michael's father, had left Santa Barbara minutes before and were now also on their way south to the larger airport.

Once in Panama, the families traveled to the resort city of

Boquete, as close to the airport at David as they could get. On Monday morning, Christmas Eve, an early attempt at a search had been called off because of the weather. Later that morning, another airplane tried to take off but came back because of driving rain, fog, and high winds. Several friends who were bush pilots flew down to try to assist the families.

The terrain in the interior of Panama is dense jungle, with mountains rising to thirty-five hundred feet.

Anxiety gripped me. It was a different kind of worry from anything I had felt before. It was as if I were almost feeling what Val was feeling. Almost. It was the not knowing. The feeling was intolerable. And then I felt my own feeling: helplessness. Nothing I could do from so far away. Should my husband and I get on a plane and go down to join a search party? (The heroic response, but the rational reply would be, *You don't really speak Spanish, Nora, and you can't fly a plane or even read a compass. A lot of help you would be.*) And then I realized that Val, too, must feel helpless. This woman who had protected her daughters at a party must be insane with helplessness.

The four of us ate our breakfasts and then stood up to leave. Jodie promised to keep in touch, and my husband and I went home. My husband's family was in town for the holiday. There were presents still to be wrapped. Chicken chili stew to be prepared for a light dinner after the early service at church. Ornaments to be put out for trimming the tree later. *The weather was bad, the ceiling low, so the search planes could not take off.*

No news as the day wore on.

And so at three thirty, I drove over to the hotel to pick up my mother-in-law, Peggy, and take her to church. She and I have this little routine over the holidays. We go to the early service, the "children's Christmas Eve service," because we've grown fond of watching the kids act out the Christmas story. Then we can go back to our house and settle in, trim the tree, and go to bed early. Peggy was dressed and ready; she asked me if there had been any more news and told me the story was on TV. We drove to church.

My church, Trinity Episcopal Church in Santa Barbara's downtown, is a Gothic pile of yellow sandstone, designed by the same architect who built the National Cathedral.

It was quiet as we walked up the steps and greeted the ushers. I found us a pew toward the front of the church so we'd have a good view of the pageant to come. As I settled Peggy into her seat, I looked up and saw a girl Frankie's age talking to her mother, her face that particular twelve-year-old girl combination of child and teenager, still with the childlike vulnerability and openness not yet covered over with a teenage mask, and I burst into tears. I stood there, and what had been lying under everything all day came up to the fore. *I can't pray*, I thought. *I have so much anxiety that I can't find my way through to pray. I don't even know how to pray. What should I pray for? Who should I pray for?*

Frankie, stay with the plane, I had thought earlier in the day. Was that a prayer? I stood there, crying, and then I saw Eva, our associate priest, walking across the altar area. I found myself leaving the pew and walking toward her.

"Eva," I said.

"Oh, hi," she said, in that tone that says, *I've got about two minutes.*

"Eva, a friend's daughter is missing in a plane, a crash probably. Will you pray for her? I don't know how." And I cried again.

"Oh, no," she said. "Oh, of course I will. And I suppose, well, I guess it's not too good a time, but I was going to ask you to help with Communion because we're missing a LEM." (A Lay Eucharist Minister helps with Communion by serving the wine.)

Something stirred in me. "I can do that," I said, and immediately regretted it. I was hardly in a state to serve the wine. I almost said, "Oh, sorry, no I can't," but she was turning away; she had a lot of work to do. I didn't see anyone in the near vicinity who could take my place. I walked back to the pew.

The choir began to sing "O Come, All Ye Faithful," and everyone stood up. The kids brought in a wood cradle and put it near the altar. Two kids, around fourteen—Mary in a pair of jeans and a blue scarf over her head and Joseph, a skinny boy with dark hair—came in and stood near it. They both looked as if, should they accidentally touch each other, they would both scream. A flock of angels, ages three to four, with gauzy wings walked up the aisle and floated around Mary and Joseph, weakly flapping their arms. They'd flap and then forget and sort of stand there; one held her thumb firmly in her mouth. Their mothers prompted them in stage whispers. "Fly, fly," one mother said, flapping her own arms. Her little girl smiled and said, "Mama!"

Then we got to the point in the service when Eva lifted up the bread and wine and said, "The gifts of God for the people of God." That was my cue, and I walked up to the altar to receive the wine and bread. Then I took a goblet of wine from one of the acolytes and started to serve.

It is always its own thing, serving the wine. Once when I served the wine, I saw the mark of lips on the cup just before I wiped it off, and I thought how the trace of our lips on the cup are the traces of human on the infinite, a fragile moment recorded, and then time moves on.

"The blood of Christ," I said to Elaine, who is ninety-five, a former dancer. "The cup of salvation." She looked at me as she received, and she placed her hand on my arm.

"The blood of Christ," I said to my mother-in-law, who held my sleeve. The tears were running down my cheeks, and there was nothing I could do about them.

And then, all of a sudden, I got it. I got what I needed to know that day.

Holy Communion was a web, a web of people who were being stitched together. And tomorrow, we would need to be stitched together again. Over and over. One person to the next. And I, today, was doing the stitching. In my weakened, anxious, weepy state, along with another chalice minister, who was working next to me, I was making basting stitches, the kind I learned in home economics from Mrs. Davis in seventh grade. Nothing fancy, nothing permanent.

> *Holy Communion was a web, a web of people being stitched together. And tomorrow, we would need to be stitched together again.*

A little boy dropped his bread on the floor, and his mother picked it up and without a moment's hesitation popped it into her mouth. I missed the right placement on a gray-haired woman and touched her lips with my finger, and she frowned. A guy tried to dip his own bread and got his finger in the wine, and I wanted to smack him. Here we were: the rough material.

And then it was over. I went back to the pew and sat down next to my mother-in-law. She patted my hand. I wept and wept and wept. Then we stood to sing "Silent Night" and we walked out into the chilly December air.

Just as we got back to our house, Jodie called. The rain was still falling in Panama, and visibility remained low. Val and Kirk and the Klein family had organized a search party to comb the area where the plane was last seen. A map had been drawn up, and the area had been divided into sectors. Kim Klein had offered twenty-five thousand dollars to anyone who could find the plane.

As many as fifty people set out on Tuesday morning at 4:00 a.m.

Christmas Day. We opened our stockings and gifts. The family sat around for a while, then decided to go over and visit another distant family member in town for the holidays. I declined. Suddenly, more than anything, what I needed was sleep. I lay down on the window seat in our dining room, with the kitty lying on my legs, and the two of us went out like lights. *Frankie*, I thought, *stay with the plane.*

My cell phone was ringing. Where was it?

"They found the plane," Jodie said, and she started to cry. "There is one survivor. They think it's Frankie."

I fell to my knees on my dining room floor.

A practice is something we do that is always the same and always different. In the world we live in, we do things over and over so we can get better at them—better at soccer, playing the piano, selling software, things that have measurable scorecards. But that is not what a spiritual practice is.

That Christmas afternoon, I was in great need. And I understood that Holy Communion was about stitching people together. I needed to be stitched together myself. It was not the kind of stitching that would last forever. It was more like what my father said when he did a job that was only temporary: "That's Scotch tape and baling wire, but it will do for now."

2

COMMUNION IS A PRACTICE

Two months after liberation, people had stopped cheering and embracing.
They had stopped giving away food and had started selling it on the black
market. Those who had compromised their integrity during the Occupation,
now began to calculate and plan, to watch and spy on each other, to cover
their tracks. . . . It was becoming evident to many that while evil grows all
by itself, good can be achieved only through hard struggle and maintained
only through tireless effort . . .

—HEDA KOVALY, *UNDER A CRUEL STAR: A LIFE IN PRAGUE, 1941–1968*

TRINITY EPISCOPAL, MY CHURCH, HAS TWO SERVICES ON
Sunday at which Communion is celebrated and served, one on
Tuesday and Thursday evenings, and one on Friday at noon.
Many of the Roman Catholic churches in my town serve
Communion every morning. (The Roman Catholic Church
has rules against someone like me taking Communion because
I am not a member; but in France, in a small village I won't
name, I asked the small, round priest in my incredibly broken
French if I, being not a Catholic and an American, could take

Communion. I gestured to myself, and to the wider space with its old, gray walls and its ancient pews. I said, brokenly, that I was only there for a month, intimating that by the time the religious police arrived, I'd be gone. He practically winked and replied, more or less, "The farther from Rome, the less the rules count.")

> *Communion goes on all over the world in many churches*
> *in different languages but in much the same form.*

Communion goes on all over the world in many churches in different languages but in much the same form. In France, I could follow it even though I was in a Roman Catholic church and the words were in, yes, French. When they served Communion, two altar boys stood on either side of the priest and held a piece of linen so white it hurt my eyes, to catch Jesus if they dropped him. In Prague, I attended a service of the Church of England where, at the exchange of the peace, the men and women held their hands out in front of them as if to barricade themselves from a possible American hug, but the Communion service was more or less the same. In Nicaragua, women and their babies practically danced to the altar to receive Communion, while a salsa band played and a German TV crew stuck a camera in my face, but we were all eating the bread and drinking the wine. In Ireland, where no slight or crime is forgotten, I asked a hotel clerk where the Church of England was, and she pointed in the general direction of north. Then she said, "But if you want to go to a *real* church . . ."

The monks at an Episcopal monastery in the hills above Santa Barbara gathered every day at noon to celebrate Communion. (Holy Cross Monastery burned down in 2008.) I have been there with them. I know how the quiet of their chapel came over you as you walked in the door, like the relief you felt after having finished something hard. They stood in a half circle around the small altar of stone in white robes (which they'd thrown over jeans and gardening clothes and cook's aprons, with their running shoes poking out from underneath) and sang, sometimes off-key. Even when I didn't attend, I was consoled that they were there. When I thought about why, the image I had was from an old child's story—somewhere someone's grandmother may be spinning or knitting the fate of the whole world, without anyone knowing it, even the one who does it. It's the same feeling I have when someone says about some small endangered animal that it doesn't count, it has no worth. "Why should we care?" they say. And my reply is, "How do we know?" Without that animal, the natural world may start to unravel; without these monks, what we think of as the world of the spirit might begin to fray.

On those days when I have thought of giving up on church entirely, I have tried to figure out what I would do about Communion. I could not just pass my hand over some bread and wine and then drink it by myself.

And neither can a priest or minister. One Thursday evening,

when our head priest, Mark Asman, was presiding at the service, he said to the four or five of us gathered there, "Would you come a little closer? I can't do this by myself, you know."

He really cannot do it alone. Communion is not Communion without two or three "gathered in my name" (Matthew 18:20). It does not rest on an individual; it is not a priest's magic act.

Communion is therefore, of necessity, a communal activity. It's unlike every other Christian practice in that sense. Communion is meant to be done together; it has to be done in community. You can pray alone and fast alone. You can even go on pilgrimage alone. But you can't take Communion alone. More than any other practice, taking Communion forces us to be with others, to stand with them in a circle or kneel at the altar rail or pass a tray of grape juice and cubes of bread. We are forced to be with strangers and people we don't like, persons of different colors and those with bad breath or breathing cheap alcohol. (I once served the cup to the last guy in line, who was dressed in rags, and he drained it dry.) It forces "them" to be with "us" and us to be with them. Communion is, more than any other practice, a humbling experience. We are stuck with each other, at that altar, for at least a few minutes.

Communion is meant to be done together; it has to be done in community.

I remember quite keenly the Sunday morning I stood up from my pew and marched toward the altar without really paying attention to who was with me in the line. I think I was imagining a new haircut or the perfect apartment in New York, my two favorite fantasies. When I got to the altar and took my place in the circle, my knuckles knocked against those of a person standing right next to me. When I glanced over, I saw a woman I was not speaking to. We both gave a little start, and I felt immediate shame. I could remember exactly why we were not talking and everything *she* had done to cause it; but I realized, as I stood there with about an inch of ice-cold space between us, that I had done exactly nothing to make things even the smallest bit better. *Ha!* the Spirit must have been saying over us. *Let's see what happens now.*

In a world of gated communities and single cars and large houses, it's not easy to find yourself next to someone you dislike. We used to run into everyone in the whole village just about every day—at the well, in the fields, or even asleep right next to you in a big, warm pile of bodies. I am grateful for the amount of privacy our greater wealth gives us, but it comes at a price. Every effort to make amends has to be so self-conscious, so planned, that it's almost impossible for any animal as proud as we are. It's almost easier, I saw that day, to have your nemesis foisted on you. At least, at a minimum, you'll get used to her smell.

And Communion is all about the body. Every ancient practice is bodily, but this one is very, very much so. You have to move and open your mouth and hold out your hands. It is the one practice that is really about ingesting spirit, eating what we call God but what may as well be called taking a bite out of infinity.

Communion is all about the body.

Holy Communion has had a lot of bad press. Many church fathers, and probably a bunch of church mothers, have contributed to making Communion one of the most mystifying and obscure aspects of Christianity and larded it with rules and regulations and arguments over whether it's really, really the body and blood of Christ or really, really not—whether it's the Real Presence or only a symbol. Also, there has been much arguing over who gets to take it and which sins and transgressions will keep you from the altar. If you Google "Holy Communion" or "Eucharist," you will see what I mean. Centuries of people parsing, speculating, opining, and above all, fighting. Just what Jesus had in mind.

Put aside all the arguments and rules and debates about whether the elements of Communion are actually Christ's body and blood or the Real Presence for a little while. I'll get to it, but for now, just place it over there where you can see it but don't have to think about it.

In these pages, I hope to clarify Communion and give you just enough of its history and tradition that you will understand where it's been in the last two thousand years—but not so much as to make you run screaming from the room. (Cartoon: Jesus, trailing a huge cloud of things—books, poems, paintings, plays, movies—walks up to God and says, "Look, Dad, what followed me home. Western civilization!" And God says, "You can't keep that. You don't know where it's been.")

More than anything, I want to introduce Communion to you as a practice. As something for you, devised cleverly by and for human beings, to help us get in touch with the holy. Because so much has been written about it, Communion's identity as a practice is obscured; it's not, after all, surprising that I didn't think of it as one. It's thought of as an odd ritual by some, and as the holy center of the church service by others, but it is not often pictured in the same world as prayer or fasting or pilgrimage. But like these other practices, Communion has the same intention: to gradually move us out of one place and into another.

> *Like these other spiritual practices, Communion has the same intention: to gradually move us out of one place and into another.*

I opened this chapter with a quote from Heda Kovaly's extraordinary memoir about her life in Prague after surviving Auschwitz. "Evil grows all by itself," Kovaly wrote, having watched what happened in her city a few months after the Nazi surrender, "while good is achieved only through hard struggle and maintained through tireless effort."[1]

This is unfair: the chances of doing good or doing evil in a life should at least be fifty-fifty, but apparently, and from my own experience, that's not the case. On a sliding scale, I tend toward the same narcissism that seems to drive many of us. Put me in a traffic jam, and I'm the one screaming at the suddenly slowed-down driver, not the one who guesses that the poor woman has missed her exit and is trying to figure out what to do next. Or worse, when the company I work for laid off 20 percent of its employees in 1991, I hid my face from those who got pink slips.

If "evil" and "good" are too abstract, let's substitute a few more concrete words: What do you *think* about all day? What do you desire? Do you give yourself enough *time* to let your heart fill with compassion, or are you, like me, too *busy*?

It's complex, this business of living the right kind of life. The three Abrahamic faiths have been wrestling with how to do it for much longer than two thousand years, and the many faiths that preceded them struggled with it as well.

Even with rich stories and wise guides, all of us religious people have often focused on just the wrong way to make the right life. Obey this set of rules, we've said from pulpits and in Sunday schools, and everything will work out perfectly for you. If you tithe to the church and attend every Sunday and say the Lord's Prayer before you go to bed, you'll be fine. Or if you do what the priest or minister says, then you'll be rewarded. Keep your head down and don't get into trouble, and you will come out okay. The problem with this kind of religious practice is that it isn't about God; it's about an institution's longing to keep itself going, our desire to fit in, and expecting this effect from this cause. We mistake middle-class conventions or church rules or traditions for the secret code that unlocks the kingdom.

> *We mistake middle-class conventions or church rules*
> *or traditions for a secret code that unlocks the kingdom.*

Here's how I imagine it: You may recall the story in Luke, chapter 7, about the so-called notorious woman. That story opens with a dinner party, a public sort of dinner party, not exactly like one we might attend in a private home but perhaps more like a present-day art opening or fund-raiser where there are invited guests and also people coming in off the street. The invited guests are, one assumes, all men. Enter an unnamed, notorious woman who cries all over Jesus' feet, then dries them with her hair and anoints them with expensive oil.

One can only imagine the horror on the faces of the invited guests.

They thought to be faithful to God was to be upright. Nice men all dressed up in dark suits and ties, ready to settle down to a good meal of spring lamb and baby organic vegetables and listen to what this nice young teacher has to say. And afterward, each one of them planned to go home and kiss his wife and children and go on living exactly as he had before.

The stories that Jesus tells were more often than not about people who broke the religious rules, not simply for the sake of breaking them, but for something bigger, more important, more life-giving. The notorious woman. The Samaritan woman whose daughter was possessed by demons. The woman caught in adultery. Tax collectors. And Jesus himself broke the rules by healing on the Sabbath, eating with those who were unclean, and resisting the power of the Roman Empire until he got himself into real trouble.

Jesus grew up under the heel of an empire. And he saw, all around him, its cost. The Romans saw themselves as creating a new world order. To accomplish this, Roman soldiers burned villages, pillaged the countryside, and slaughtered or enslaved those they conquered. Huge taxes were imposed on the people in the colonies. When the Roman governor Antipas built two Roman-style cities in Galilee, a rural countryside, the Galilean peasants had to provide the resources for the Romans' massive building project. They paid taxes unto Caesar.

We don't know exactly how Jesus fits into this reality, but to imagine that he was not influenced by his place in time, or had nothing to say about it, is more than far-fetched.

How does this speak to us, today? We know from his life that Jesus chose not to identify with those with power. There are no Gospel stories about Jesus having drinks at the private clubs of Antipas or Herod.

We are all, every one of us, interested in having power. Some power is good: the power to speak; the power to live out your vocation, whatever it is; the power to have what is called agency,

Pastor Dana Runestad
HOLY CROSS LUTHERAN CHURCH
30650 Six Mile Rd.
Livonia, MI 48152
(734) 427-1414   cell: (734) 765-1141
email: pastordana@holycrosslivonia.org

Pat —

Here's hoping Nora Gallagher's perspective might redeem some of that catholic upbringing you so courageously wrestle with! I treasure our friendship. Dana

the ability to act. We speak of empowerment, calling out of others their own strength and creativity. But we also know, as the adage says, that power corrupts. Even in the smallest ways, power can corrupt the work of love. We know, as Heda Kovaly wrote, that it is easier to do evil than it is to do good.

Even in the smallest ways, power can corrupt the work of love.

Many of us have been on either the giving or on the receiving end of the corruption of power. We see it in the many CEOs who have confessed to lying, cheating, and stealing. Power unabated can become demonic; witness Stalin, Hitler, Rwanda. And I think we have all, at one time or another, collaborated in the abuse of power, small and large. At my workplace, I've made sure I kept my turf intact, nurtured my ties to the owners of the company. I seek out powerful people to cozy up to. I, like just about everyone else in America, want to identify myself with those who have more, not with those who have less. Notice I said *identify* myself. I give to the poor, and I taught in a homeless shelter, but I don't identify myself with them. The people I snuggle next to are the ones with the power.

Jesus, too, faced choices between power and vulnerability. He was a man who over the short stretch of his life came into contact with power over and over again. He made choices. Once again, let's not confuse power with agency. Jesus was no passive guy, no milquetoast. He had a lot of agency, and he used it well.

But let's remember where and with whom he spent his time: Jesus took a blind man by the hand and restored his sight. He fed a crowd with loaves and fish. He helped a deaf and mute man find his voice again. He listened when a Gentile woman begged him to heal her daughter of demons. He did not even exclude persons who were collaborators with the empire, such as the tax collector Matthew. He bound himself to those in need.

Jesus' parables are as clear as water in regard to power: Don't be absorbed in who is sitting at the head of the table. The last shall be first. The meek will inherit the earth.

Early in this journey, I took these stories as difficult admonitions, slightly accusatory reminders of how I should always remember those on the margins. But what I am coming to understand is that Jesus meant to say these things to himself, as much as to me. He said these things to himself because he understood that choosing the vulnerable path was the way to keep his soul alive, and protected, from the harsh realities of power. He sought out the vulnerable because they helped keep him vulnerable. And he finally came to identify with them.

Jesus' compassion for those who suffer because of the powerful is, as the theologian Walter Brueggemann puts it, "a radical form of criticism," for it announces that "the hurt is to be taken seriously, that the hurt is not to be accepted as normal and natural but is an abnormal and unacceptable condition for humanness."[2]

Jesus, in his compassion, says that the hurt of those who are hungry and poor and taxed beyond their means is to be taken seriously. It is not normal for people to be without food; it is not normal for someone who is blind or deaf to beg on the street.

Injustice has a price, and it's paid in human flesh. Many of the men who came to the soup kitchen we operated at my church, Trinity, were homeless because the parts of town that had once been their sanctuaries were gradually redeveloped into places for time-share condos and fancy beachside hotels. The single-room-occupancy, cheap hotels downtown were sold, renovated, and became boutique spas. The people in our parish who worked at the Faulding Hotel, one of the last single-room-occupancy hotels in town, knew this story. Or we can just as well imagine the sweat shops where our T-shirts are made, or the pesticides that migrant workers have to breathe so our strawberries look nice, or the bombs and shrapnel that penetrate, as we speak, the bodies of civilians in Iraq.

Brueggemann continued, "Empires are never built nor are they maintained on the basis of compassion."[3] Empires, like Rome, like the United States, like China, live by keeping their own citizens distracted with "bread and circuses." The Roman rulers expected their citizens to remain silent in response to the human cost of war, mute in the face of the human cost of greed. And they kept those in the colonies in check by systemic terror: the price of prophetic witness was death.

But Jesus speaks up. He acts. By and through his compassion, he takes the first step in revealing, as Brueggemann says, the abnormality that has become business as usual. By healing a leper, Jesus exposes the fact that lepers are isolated and abandoned. By healing a woman who had been bleeding for years, Jesus reveals that she has been unfairly ostracized for something she did not cause and could do nothing about. By feeding the five thousand, Jesus shows everyone that people are hungry. By practicing nonviolence at every turn, Jesus unveils the violence that was the underpinning of the empire. Without violence, empires can't exist.

This led him, finally, inexorably, to the cross. To the place where power and vulnerability, where power and reality, intersect or, more accurately, collide. The cross stood at the end of a long series of choices. Like Dietrich Bonhoeffer, who decided to return to Germany from a safe haven in the United States; like Rosa Parks, who finally sat down at the front of a bus; like Martin Luther King, whose words inspired a nation; Jesus did not suddenly make a choice between power and vulnerability. He put his foot on a path, and years later he looked back and saw where that path had led him.

I remember thinking as I worked in the soup kitchen that I didn't want to know what I was learning. Because then my life couldn't go on in the same way as it had before: driving around in my nice red Volvo, thinking about what new linens to buy. What we learn we cannot unlearn; what we see, we cannot unsee.

Jesus doesn't call us to live in a soft cocoon, distracted and undisturbed, allowing others to pay the costs of our comfort.

When it comes right down to it, Jesus followed where compassion led him, and he bore the cost of what he found. Jesus asks us to follow where compassion leads, and bear the cost of what we find.

> *Jesus asks us to follow where compassion leads,*
> *and bear the cost of what we find.*

He calls us, as Nicholas Cage says in the movie *Moonstruck*, "to ruin ourselves and break our hearts and love the wrong people and die!"[4] We are invited to ruin the old life of silence, to break our hearts with compassion over suffering, to love the wrong person—that would be Jesus—and to die. As a friend of mine once said, "To get resurrected, ya gotta get dead." Because we know, from Jesus' example and from our own lives, what lies on the other side of this death. The other side of silence and distraction, of the deadly life of business as usual, is new life, resurrected life, born of compassion—awake, brokenhearted, and, yes, dangerous.

On the last night of his life, Jesus said, "Do this to remember me" (Luke 22:19 NLT). Many of us think these words, these Last Supper words, mean that we're remembering Jesus when we drink of this cup and eat of this bread. Well, of course, we're remembering Jesus, but that should not be all we're doing. I don't think Jesus was interested in everybody just remembering him. What's the point of that? That puts Jesus in the category with the various celebrities who will do anything to get into the media so we'll remember they're still alive. Instead, I think Jesus wanted his disciples and everyone who came after him to remember *what they had together*. What they made together. What it meant to be together. How the things he wanted them to do could not be done alone. How the things he did could not have been done without them.

"Do this to remember how we healed the sick, and cured the lepers and relieved those possessed by demons. Do this to remember how we were a band of men and women who traveled together and ate together and were a company of friends."

"This is my body," Jesus said, "given for you" (Luke 22:19).

Instead of thinking of that Communion as a ghoulish eating of human flesh, think of those who gather at Communion as the body of Jesus. We are the body given for each other. *This is my body*, he said. *Look around you.*

When we all show up and do our parts, we are the sacrament, the body of Christ. *Do this to remember me. Do this to remember who you were with me. Do this to remember who you are.*

> *A practice is meant to connect you with what is*
> *deeply alive, to stir in you the same kind of aliveness*
> *that the disciples of Jesus must have felt around him*

A practice is meant to connect you with what is deeply alive, to stir in you the same kind of aliveness that the disciples of Jesus must have felt around him. A practice trains and disciplines the mind to head toward compassion rather than toward greed. A practice is not about finding exactly the right set of rules that will make you "good" but is instead meant to establish a habit of connection to a world that is both tenuous and surprising, outside of time and in it. A practice is designed to train the mind to think about something other than, in my case, real estate and haircuts, and to recover the thread, the meaning.

3

WAITING

If Jesus were beside you now, gazing with compassion on the mess that you—like all of us—have sometimes made of things, what would you say to him?

—MARGARET BULLITT-JONAS, *CHRIST'S PASSION, OUR PASSION*

IF YOU ASKED ME ON SUNDAY MORNING AS I LIE IN BED, IF I want to rouse myself to eat a wafer of fish food or a little bite of probably stale bread and take a sip of fortified wine, the answer is: circle Yes or No. But once I haul myself there, I am drawn into it. I want to join the long lines of people standing in the aisle.

Taking Communion for me has three parts: waiting, receiving, and afterward. The waiting is a warming up. For me, that starts when the priest says, "The gifts of God for the people of God." Before that, I'm still in the other part of the service: what we call the liturgy of the Word: sermon, prayers, readings. In that first part of the service, I am more or less in my head. Then, as I get up from my seat and begin the walk toward the altar, I begin to be somewhere else.

As I stand behind the back in front of me, I feel as if I am about to travel into a foreign country. The language will be different. The familiar words won't do. The first time I went to Italy, some part of me was absolutely sure the Italians were just pretending they did not speak English. I kept saying, "Where is the bathroom?" and "Where is the train station?" very, *very* loudly, but, remarkably, they still shook their heads and threw up their hands. It took me a long time to figure out that they really spoke Italian, a different language, and that one of us would have to bend if we were to understand each other.

The language of the altar is old, much older than us. And it's also new, being made by you and the people around you. A world created, maybe long before time, that you step into and change. It is like stepping into a river that contains waters from its source and waters from just up the way.

That's another reason Communion is a practice. A practice is something that connects us to a world much older than ourselves, something that is re-created and made new by our participation. This other place, related to this one and intimately tied to it, may be necessary for our world's ongoing life and well-being, and you can choose to step into it or not.

The practice of Communion is meant to remind us of a place we can go that may not be always visible in daily life. And, quite often, a practice is something we don't want to do. Every time. "Why is it," the thirteenth-century Sufi poet Rumi said, "that I have to be dragged, kicking and screaming into paradise?"

The practice of Communion is meant to remind us of a place we can go that may not be always visible in daily life.

I have never quite figured this out, but I suspect that the painful part of "paradise" is the border crossing, the transition between the daily world and the world the practice leads us toward. Nobody I know likes the night before travel.

So how do we pack for this particular border crossing?

I am not a light traveler. I view those who travel light as people to be admired but not emulated. I mean, a girl needs to have choices. I am sure I will arrive in the afterlife with a bag marked "Overweight." The baggage I carry to the Communion line is not filled with clothing and shoes but instead the things stuffed into my head: worry, guilt, anxiety, way too many rationalizations.

That large suitcase of anxiety and concern is part of my waiting, part of my preparation for taking Communion. I know by now that I have to just live through it; I have to drag that piece of baggage around until it's no longer useful to me. So part of waiting is packing and repacking that bag, stuffing it with worry and pain.

Part of waiting, in many churches, is a group or solo confession. It used to be a common practice in the Roman Catholic Church to go to confession on Saturday afternoon or evening in preparing for taking Communion on Sunday. A brief confession and the Lord's Prayer are part of the service in many Episcopal churches, before Communion. I say the prayer every Sunday just like all the other people standing next to me in the pew: "Forgive us our trespasses" or "forgive us our sins," and the kicker, "as we forgive those who trespass [sin] against us." And then I hold next to my heart all the sins and trespasses I don't forgive.

Sin has almost as much bad press and bad history in churches as does Communion. Too much focus on personal sin, and especially sin having to do with sex (while many church leaders got away with serious sexual misconduct and abuse) without any mention of how we participate in larger, more systemic evil, has left the word *sin* almost empty of meaning. But one way to define sin is to ask, what separates me from God? What holds me back from connecting to and deepening my relationship with time-lessness and love? (Today, I would answer, addiction to e-mail.)

One way to define sin is to ask, what separates me from God?

But sin also has to be about larger matters. Jesus didn't spend a lot of time talking about personal conduct (obey the commandments was his general rule); his teachings were more about justice. The man had a thing about justice. Sin in this area has to do with the larger world, and our part in it. I'd like to take a look at the old biblical story of Sodom and Gomorrah for some clues about sin.

Sodom and Gomorrah were famous towns located next to each other, rather like Minneapolis and St. Paul. There are many versions of why they were eventually destroyed. Prevalent among them are sadistic cruelty to beggars and visitors, murder, greed. Jewish commentaries affirm that the Sodomites committed terrible and repeated economic crimes against each other and outsiders, including rape, both homosexual and heterosexual. Flavius Josephus, a Romano-Jewish historian, wrote, "Now, about this time the Sodomites, overwhelmingly proud of their numbers and the extent of their wealth, showed themselves insolent to men and impious to the divinity, insomuch that they no more remembered the benefits that they had received from him, hated foreigners and avoided any contact with others."[1]

Sodom, by the way, is derived from a Hebrew word meaning "burnt," and Gomorrah from a word meaning "buried," references to their destruction.

In this story, you might recall, we also have a scary view of God, a divine being who is ready to burn the cities to the ground and finally, later in the story, does just that; he smites them, leaving one man standing and his wife turned to salt.

And in the tale also, we have Abraham, who reminds God that the story of salvation is the story of individual human beings. Abraham persuades God to stay his hand on behalf of the few—they get down to ten—who are still righteous. God was ready to be just, to punish the wicked; Abraham reminds God to be merciful. That both God and Abraham should care about a single human life is more than pure sentiment. It means that a single human life is to be weighed against the aggregate, the group, the nation. Ten righteous persons have the same weight as thousands of bad ones.

The world of Sodom and Gomorrah is a good description of an empire. The two cities are proud, wealthy, inventive, rapacious, destructive, on top of the heap. They are hostile to strangers and have forgotten, as Josephus put it, "the benefits that they had received" from God. Above all, these citizens are greedy: they just can't stop themselves from wanting more. I'll bet they bought cheap clothes, made, you know, somewhere offshore, and didn't ask what the workers were paid or what went into the water. Did they employ illegal aliens to clean their houses so they didn't have to pay a living wage or benefits? And they were busy all the time, of course, with nothing left for their friends much less their families. Remind you of anyone you know? Don't worry, I'm squirming too.

We now live in a world of Sodom and Gomorrah writ large: modern industrial economic systems, especially global capitalism, are very good at the production of wealth and very bad at sustainability. The human desire for more and more, coupled with an economic machine that demands growth and profits, is outrunning the world's ability to regenerate itself. You know the litany of horrors: depleted forests, crashing stocks of fish; in 2006, the meadow bird population took a dive. Think of it! Meadow birds. Carbon emissions have heated the weather and polluted the ocean. Global warming, now an indisputable fact, not only disrupts our lives but the lives of animals and plants.

We may be in for a wave of extinctions. Bumper sticker of the year: *At least the war on the environment is going well.*

If we don't take the scary-God version of the story of Sodom and Gomorrah literally, but instead think of what this story might be saying about the nature of deep reality and about the nature of sin, then perhaps this is what happened to these two cities: they accumulated too much debt, both moral and economic. They were out of balance. And finally it came time for them to pay up. Just as the time came for Rome, and the time will come for the United States, the time will come for China, and . . . you name the country. At some point, this story says, if you break all the covenants: if you travel too far from what is balanced and sane, you just go over the edge. One day you wake up, or worse, your grandchildren wake up, and there is nothing left but weeds and rats and ashes.

What does it mean to live in this situation as a Christian? What am I, what are we, supposed to do? How does the practice of Communion help us find a better way?

In partial answer, let's go back to what Jesus emphasized. Throughout the Gospels, Jesus describes two worlds: the one in which he is living and the one that might be. Scholars like Marcus Borg and Walter Brueggemann believe that Jesus preached to and in his historical context. Living in an empire, he preached about it. He described its excesses, its inequality, its failure to take care of the vulnerable and the helpless. Jesus' compassion, as Walter Brueggemann said and I wrote earlier, is not sentimentality or simple emotion but is instead a critique of the existing order. Empires are neither built nor maintained on the basis of compassion.

Jesus' "kingdom of God" may not be a far-off heaven, but may instead be an alternative to the kingdom of Rome, an alternative to the monetary, social, moral, and legal economy of the Roman Empire and the religious authorities who collaborated with it. An alternative to waste and corruption and greed. Jesus promises us the kingdom of heaven: more compassion, more love, more spirit, more mercy, more justice, more courage, more surprise. Everything but more money.

Part of waiting to take Communion is examining how we have been like the citizens of Sodom and Gomorrah, how we have been drawn into the empire's kingdom (how we have sinned), and at the same time, to check in on how we have been like the citizens of Jesus' kingdom of God. The regular practice of Communion is meant to help move us from being the citizens of an empire to the citizens of heaven.

> *The regular practice of Communion is meant to help move us from being the citizens of the empire to the citizens of heaven.*

The bags I carry to the country of the altar are filled with anxiety and fear, competition, envy, and greed. *I want her shoes, her haircut, her face, her life. Why is her book doing better than mine? If I had what he has, then I would be happy.* They are filled with the ways in which I've neglected to see the injustices all around me, and how I've ignored my part in them.

If I did not do this practice, I would probably not even notice the bags I carry. They would just be "normal," part of the landscape. I might notice that I've put on some weight or that my feet are dragging, but I would probably just chalk it up to the ice cream I ate last night. And so, a practice, among other things, is the art of noticing: it helps us shift our perspective, from that mall of things to buy and the greed and envy we share with the citizens of Sodom and Gomorrah, to the kingdom of heaven. It's almost imperceptible, but when I remember to look, to shift my gaze from the mall to the kingdom, I feel as if I have discovered an antidote to poison. And what do I see when I see the kingdom of heaven? I see the violet swallows that zing through the air around my cousin's cabin in the mountains, switching course on a dime. I see the rather handsome young black bear I met on the trail up there that stood off to the side and watched me for a minute or two while I watched him. (I thought we were communing; he probably was thinking about whether I was worth eating.) I see the lilies of the field and the birds of the air. I see God's extraordinary and beautiful creation. I see people who live with restraint. I see poets and painters, unsung and unpaid, who bring me a dose of freedom and beauty. I see the power of subversive inspiration. I see a world where you can never tell what will make the final difference, what will add just enough weight to the scales to tip them, so people just keep plugging along.

Sometimes I even see what saved my life today, what made my life worth living. It is a world that is fragile and always at risk. Especially now. But Jesus puts great faith in that kingdom. Or to put it another way, he puts great faith in us. Jesus puts great faith in our ability to change course, to answer his call.

> *Jesus puts great faith in our ability to change course, to answer his call.*

Abraham argues with God about Sodom and Gomorrah. He asks God if he will stay his hand if Abraham can find fifty righteous people. And when God says yes, he asks him if maybe twenty-five will do. And so on, until they get down to ten. Only ten righteous people.

It may take only ten people left to remind us of how to save our lives and what it is to be human. And the attributes of those ten people would be different. One will keep her compassion alive by caring for men and women dying of HIV/AIDS. One will be so courageous and steadfast she will stand on a corner at noon protesting the horror of war. One will start a soup kitchen. One will make of his work as the director of a funeral home a ministry of compassion and caring. Another will stop driving once a week, and change to energy-saving lightbulbs. And there will be others, who choose not to live lives of insolence and greed, but cause us to remember what the kingdom of heaven looks like, what a human being is really made of, what a citizen can be. And the rest of us may be saved by them, because they kept alive so much that when it comes time to take our turn at the wheel, we will know by their examples what to do.

So part of waiting in Communion is examining what we did last week to find the kingdom of heaven in our midst and to help others find it. I urge you to go both easy and hard on yourself in this regard. You can't just condemn yourself for not doing enough. Join the crowd. None of us does enough. I think it's important to find the things you did do and honor yourself for them, small as they might be.

Remember, you will never know what tips the scales, how each individual action adds to the whole. In Czechoslovakia, it took years of men and women refusing to comply with the secret police, signing petitions, writing letters, even going to prison. Nothing happened or nothing seemed to happen for years. The change was slow but inexorable. It accumulated. No one could see it exactly. In the winter of 1989, things began to move. Students protested. The police suppressed them. The next day, more people showed up. On November 19, two hundred thousand people protested in the city's main square. The next day, a woman from Prague, a family therapist, told me she was driving in the city to pick up her husband and saw all of these people gathered. "Suddenly," she said, "I decided to get out of my car and join them." Hundreds of thousands of people made the same decision. They arrived at the square. Now there were five hundred thousand. They shook bells and car keys at the Communist leader. He was gone within a week, and the Communist Party rule over Czechoslovakia was over.

> *Part of waiting in Communion is examining what we did last week to find the kingdom of heaven in our midst and to help others find it.*

This is how change happens. One step at a time. One prayer at a time. One wafer and one cup at a time. That's why Communion is called a "practice." We are all practicing together to become more and more the makers of the kingdom that is both under our feet and right around the corner.

4

RECEIVING

When I slowed down, I could feel my pulse beating under my chin, like a small bird nestled against my neck. The girdle of my diaphragm loosened, causing great sighs too deep for words to pour from my body. In their wake, I discovered more room around my heart, a greater capacity for fresh air.

—BARBARA BROWN TAYLOR, *LEAVING CHURCH*

THE ACT OF RECEIVING IS NOT SOMETHING MANY OF US, especially in religious circles, spend much time training to do. Talk to us all day long about sacrifice, sin, and retribution, but receiving? Getting something for nothing? Not on the list.

I like watching other people open presents, but I am awkward at my own birthday parties. If I am the center of attention because I have earned it, then it's okay, but if it's just my *birthday*?

Working hard for what you get is ingrained in our psyches; it's the advice we give to children and students, the very basis of the American dream. We tell ourselves that there's no such thing as a free lunch, that we have to work hard to get what we want.

I know a bishop who said that right after he was elected,

he drove all over his diocese in northern Minnesota, listening to educational tapes. Bob Anderson felt it was important to be an educated and up-to-date bishop. And when he got to the church he was visiting, he said, he would basically disgorge onto the people everything he had just learned. From the looks on people's faces, he got the feeling this wasn't working.

One morning, as he was driving, he saw ahead of him a shape on the road. Drawing closer, he saw it was a box turtle. He braked, got out, picked up the turtle, and placed him safely on the other side. As he continued to visit parishes, he started keeping his eye out for turtles, and there were a lot of them, on or near the roads, in need of rescue. It became his practice to watch for them, and to stop and pick them up if they needed help.

After a while, he stopped listening to the tapes because he might miss a turtle, and he started leaving the windows open so he could smell the air, especially in the early summer. Bob discovered that he was more relaxed and attentive when he arrived at a parish, and this was what people needed and wanted rather than his version of the latest theology.

I read a story in the *New York Times* about couples who share childcare and household duties exactly fifty-fifty, in an effort to take some of the burden off women, who, according to most recent statistics, still do 75 percent of childcare and housekeeping even when working full-time. One man who shared childcare with his wife had a job that allowed him to work fewer hours per week and take Fridays off. When he decided to leave that job and find another, he first mentioned in his résumé that, while he was determined to be a productive worker, he also shared childcare and liked to be with his children. He would therefore need to work flexible hours or a shorter workweek. He got no response to that résumé. So he decided not to mention his need for flexible hours in order to be with his children in his résumé, but talk about it in his first interviews. He got plenty of responses to his résumé, but when he talked about sharing childcare and needing flexible hours in the early interview, the companies would not go for it. Finally, he decided to wait until a company actually offered him a job to mention childcare. He finally arrived at an agreement and a job that worked out.

Bob Anderson's story is about letting go of being rewarded only for effort. But let's not make it an easy story. It's not easy to give up the status of being the most educated, up-to-date bishop. The model for being valued in this society is produce, produce, produce. We pay lip service to other values, including rest and equal parenting, but consider the experience of the shared-work father. It was almost impossible for him to get a job when equal childcare was one of his stated objectives. And I wonder what would have happened to Bishop Anderson had he run for bishop in another diocese and placed on his résumé that he liked picking up turtles?

By making our greatest and most important goal the one of productivity, we miss out on the ways that God's gifts of grace come to us by doing nothing.

> *By making our greatest and most important goal the one of productivity, we miss out on the ways that God's gifts of grace come to us by doing nothing.*

"Boy," a massage therapist said to me several weeks ago, "you sure have a lot going *out*. What's coming *in*?" Even when seeking words for rest, we use phrases like *refueling* or *recharging*, more appropriate to machines than to persons. We think the opposite of productivity is failure or laziness or, worse, irrelevance. Or, in our culture, the opposite of production is consumption. But the opposite of producing may be more like . . . stopping. When a friend of mine told her Buddhist yoga teacher that she found herself trying hard all the time, he said, "Don't."

I don't want to be cute about what happens when you stop. It's not all sudden roses and rest. When I decided to take a Sabbath from e-mail on the weekends, I must have thought about e-mail every five minutes. (I mentioned the addiction earlier, did I not?) And when I wasn't thinking about e-mail, I was worrying about what I would do with all that free time.

I don't think I'm alone, at least I hope I'm not, in being afraid of time opening up before me with nothing to fill it. When I was a kid, my mother greeted me when I came home from school and then waved good-bye as I went out into the world. Sometime around supper, I returned.

In the hours between, I let things come my way. I crawled

around in the field of alfalfa that grew next door; I lay on the back of my horse, bareback, with my arms around his big palomino neck. I fished for crawdads in the irrigation ditch. I played various improvised games with the two guys who lived around the corner. I figured out how to siphon water from a fish pond I made with my father. I ate wild rhubarb that grew in a vacant lot. I read and read and read, sometimes lying on the branch of a cottonwood tree.

"What did you do?" my mother would ask when I got home.

"Oh, nothing," I would reply.

What I know now is that I was living then in the eternal present. And I remember the very last time I felt that way for a whole afternoon: I was around thirty-five, and I was with two of my cousins, ages six and nine. We had no plan, no schedule. As we tossed coins into a fountain and wandered around in the dusty reaches of a vacant lot, I felt time dissolve. I did not think about the future. In fact, the future did not exist. That was exactly twenty-three years ago. Just as vacant lots have disappeared from our lives, so has the ability to inhabit time by "wasting it." That, my friends, is a sad commentary on our lives and, I would add, on our spiritual lives. I knew a man who was given a terminal diagnosis, who made of it an awakening. He lived every day as if it were his last, and he felt more alive than he had in years. He felt flooded with grace. Several months later, he went to his doctor to check on a recent test, and when he saw her face, he tried to stop her from speaking because he knew what she was going to say. "You're in remission," she said. "There is no sign of the cancer." And he felt the air of freedom suck right out of him as he tumbled back into the world of making plans.

Receiving at the altar is an invitation to inhabit the present. And the way in is not to try so hard. When my friend Kay moved to the Los Angeles area from Colorado, her best friend, Lucy, invited her to church. Kay sat in the back for many months, annoying Lucy with questions. "Why do you kneel?" "What's the priest doing with the bread and the cup?" When it came time for Communion, all the others rose and walked forward to receive it, but Kay sat still with her arms crossed.

After a long time, maybe six weeks, the rector walked toward her after church with his hands on his hips and his glasses pulled down to the end of his nose. He peered at Kay and asked, "Why don't you come to Communion?" in a tone that implied she was missing something. Kay mumbled something like, "I don't know," to which he replied, "This is our family, and this is our table. You should come."

Kay says it never occurred to her that she was the only person not coming forward to receive, that she stood out so vividly. His analogy to the family appealed to her, but she didn't go to Communion the next week either.

Lucy finally asked her, "What are you afraid of?" And that stung her. So she walked up to the altar, knelt, and watched as the priest came closer and closer with a little silver bowl full of disks of something "resembling Styrofoam."

Kay recalls, "It was at this point that I realized I would have to open my hands. When the moment came, I came as close as I ever have to hearing the voice of God. I heard an almost audible, *Come on, girlfriend. Open your hands.*"

Open your hands. That's easy, right? All you have to do is, duh, put your hands out in front of you and open them up. And when I did that, sitting here at my computer keyboard (and I suggest you try it right now), I got dizzy with vulnerability. My hands, hovering over my keyboard, fingers facing away from me, palms up, were those of a supplicant. I remembered the first and only time I stole something from a store, a piece of firecracker hard candy, on a dare, when I was twelve. The storekeeper caught me, of course, and he asked to see my hands. Oh, Lord. I kept one of them in a fist until he called my mother.

It's dangerous, opening your hands. You don't know what will end up in them. This may have been the smartest thing Jesus ever did. He must have thought, *How can I make them step into the unknown? How can I get them to let in some surprise? I know, I'll figure out a way for them to put their hands out in front of them, empty.*

If we did nothing else, if nothing was placed in our hands, we would have done two-thirds of what needed to be done. Which is to admit that we simply do not have all the answers; we simply do not have all the power. It is, as the saying goes, "out of our hands."

When I get to the altar and open my hands, the "redemptive wrestling" that I mentioned earlier, the doubt and faith and the wrestling between the two, the stretching and pulling, like making taffy, are right there, invisible, in my hands. So are the anxiety, the fear, the gripes, the sins, the depression, the worry—they're all there too. The cold nod to my husband, the gossip about a friend. All of the invisible baggage. These are not "given up," so much as they are released. If anything, it is like moments in other practices: like the moment in yoga when you can't bend forward one more inch, and you struggle and sweat and then, having given up, you feel the smallest amount of space, a slight opening. Like the second in meditation when you can't sit still one more minute, and then, suddenly, you fall into a larger silence than the one you were trying so hard to make for yourself.

Faith is a catch-and-release sport. And standing at the altar receiving the bread and wine is the release part.

> *Faith is a catch-and-release sport. And standing at the*
> *altar receiving the bread and wine is the release part.*

But what is it, exactly, that we are receiving in Communion?

Twenty-five years ago, my friend Harriet left her husband only weeks before Thanksgiving. It had been brewing for a long time, and although it was not the best timing in the world, the time had come. So, that year, her children went to her husband's family for the holiday, and Harriet notified her friends that she would not be celebrating. She would lie low and get through it. A friend invited her over and Harriet accepted, but they both said there would be no festive feast. Harriet arrived at her friend's house, walked outside, and was standing in the backyard when she looked up and saw a large white thing falling out of the sky toward her. It landed a few feet away from her shoes. It was—I am not kidding—a large white goose, dead as a doornail, probably shot by a hunter some miles away. Harriet stood there, dumbfounded, and then, being who she is, picked it up and called out to her friend, "We're having Thanksgiving after all."

In her talk "My Stroke of Insight," Jill Bolte Taylor, a neuroscientist who worked at Harvard's brain research center, describes watching herself have a stroke. It happened when she was thirty-seven, in the early morning. She woke up with a severe headache, and things went from bad to worse. For hours that morning, she tried to figure out how to use the telephone to get help (the numbers didn't make sense), but she also experienced intense joy and felt deeply joined to everything. She says, "My perception of physical boundaries was no longer limited to where my skin met air."[1]

Dr. Taylor reiterates what has been known for some time, that the two sides of the brain are completely different. In her case, her left brain was damaged but her right brain was intact. The left brain is about ego, reason, and language. The right brain? Imagination, creativity, empathy; and timelessness. That morning, Taylor says,

The cells in my left brain became nonfunctional because they were swimming in a pool of blood, they lost their ability to inhibit the cells in my right hemisphere. In my right brain, I shifted into the consciousness of the present moment. I was in the right here, right now awareness, with no memories of my past and no perception of the future. The beauty of La-la land (my right hemisphere experience of the present moment) was that everything was an explosion of magnificent stimulation and I dwelled in a space of euphoria.[2]

Her story is moving evidence that the brain is wired to experience some other kind of time, and another kind of connection.

At the altar, we are invited into what Jesus called heaven. It is a place that is always there, although it doesn't seem that way to us. My left brain questions its reality at the same time my right brain is leaning toward it. Countless people have described heaven by saying, "I can't describe it."

At the altar, we are invited into what Jesus called heaven.

One Christmas Eve, Mark Asman, my rector, asked me to serve the bread at Communion. I figured I would be safely tucked away at the back of the church for one of the largest services of the year, but at the rehearsal for the service, Mark marched me over to where I was to stand: smack in front of the altar. I began to panic about then. I had worn what I hoped was modest, plain garb, a gray silk blouse and skirt with a black velvet coat over it. Just before the service began, I sat down in a pew near the altar, next to a woman in a wheelchair with a partially paralyzed face. She must have had a stroke. Even taking the stroke into account, she seemed somewhat cold and stiff. Her husband was very loving. The church was packed with people I didn't know.

When it came time for Communion, I got up and took the plate stacked with wafers from the acolyte and walked over to stand in front of the altar. I felt very much alone, without much to do. But gradually, the people starting coming forward, one by one. Serving the bread is much slower than serving the wine. I held the thin piece of wafer up to each person and said, "The body of Christ. The bread of heaven." I looked in their eyes, unless they seemed to want not to look at anyone. They looked into my eyes. It was like a long gaze across a great gap, with the body of Christ in between us.

After a little while, a very short little while, I felt a small thrill of joy wash through me. I held the wafer up to a homeless man with no fingers on one hand and said, "The body of Christ. The bread of heaven," and then placed the wafer in his palm. His eyes were bright with tears. He stepped aside. The woman with the partially paralyzed face rolled forward in her wheelchair, her husband pushing her. I looked in her eyes as I tucked the wafer into the hand bent in her lap and saw that all of her life was in her eyes, and they were laughing.

Gradually, I saw that everyone was picking up on this feeling, whatever it was. Their eyes grinned. One of them almost giggled. Serving each person became a little dance step, as if we were in a minuet, or one of those dances that involves a bow and a change of partners. A choir member, a child, a teenager with a tongue stud, a tattooed man, a woman with a haggard face and too much lipstick, the joy was all around us, running through us, and we were all a part of it, we were riding in it, we were dancing through it. I knew it was going on all the time and we were, that night, invited into it; we were adding to its strength.

5

AFTERWARD

I do not at all understand the mystery of grace—only that it meets us where we are but does not leave us where it found us.

—ANNE LAMOTT, *TRAVELING MERCIES*

AFTER THAT CHRISTMAS EVE COMMUNION, I WENT BACK TO my pew and sat down. It was a short distance and a long way away. What I wanted was to stay in the feeling of being part of something that was moving and in which I was still and without anxiety. I wanted to live in that great dance all the time, as I felt once in Italy on a day when the light was perfect on the olive trees and the old, beautiful villas were shining in the sun, and someone handed me the best cappuccino I had ever tasted.

Of course, when we suddenly think, *I want to live here all the time,* whatever it was disappears. It evaporated as I sat there, and I was left with jet lag.

I wondered whether what I had experienced during Communion was real. Did I make it up? Maybe I had. I looked over at the woman in the wheelchair, in the hope of finding a corroborator. She was asleep.

I sat there alone, aching to return to paradise, with only a memory of its grandeur and possibility, and disappointed, oh, very disappointed that it was over.

Afterward. The time spent after. What I had experienced had happened in silence, and in silence, I sat there. I know people who hear words when they hear God, but perhaps because I must deal with words every day—they are the tools of my craft—my experiences of God are without them.

Something had happened to me during Communion. It was important—I would say crucial—to me, this maker of words or the finder of words, to describe for myself what felt profound about it. (Was it like crossing over a threshold? Was it inhabiting a world, related but distinct?) But the part I wanted to keep was that it happened in the midst of so many people, in the act of Communion, the night before Christmas.

> *Was Communion, I wondered, what Jesus invented to give us a preview of what the kingdom of heaven could be like?*

Was Communion, I wondered, what Jesus invented to give us a preview of what the kingdom of heaven could be like? He who told great stories, who understood the power of words, said this kingdom would be like the slacking of thirst, the miracle of a mustard seed, as easy as the lives of lilies. He must have known what he meant when he said, "Do this to remember me" (1 Corinthians 11:24 NLT).

I went recently to the annual celebration of the festival of Sukkot, the Jewish ritual of the harvest. It was held on the grounds of a Catholic retreat center near Santa Barbara. The center had been the property of the Sisters of the Immaculate Heart, a Catholic order that took Pope John XXIII's reforms and reforming spirit seriously and stopped wearing the habit in the sixties—and for their seriousness were invited to leave the Church. A few of the sisters were there, grayheaded and still stubborn, to celebrate this festival with members of B'nai B'rith temple and the university's Jewish congregations.

We gathered around a little shack with a roof of palm branches built out on the retreat's lawn under California live oaks. It was about twenty feet square. When I walked into it, I was reminded of the shelters I built as a child: some along riverbanks and on beaches, out of whatever was at hand: dead branches or driftwood or old boards. My father and I once made an igloo. I remembered how satisfying it was to walk (or more usually, crawl) into them and inhabit my work. When I visited Mesa Verde, the ancient site of (probably) Anasazi Native Americans, in the Four Corners of the Southwest, and saw their beautiful dwellings made of slivers of stone laid one on top of the other that had lasted thousands of years, I felt a thrill of recognition. They were a whole lot more proficient at building than I was as a child—they had to be—but we both had been in the same building trade, using what was at hand for material.

The Sukkot shelters are meant to be built outside, in a backyard, or out in the country, and they are meant to be temporary. Arthur Gross-Schaefer, the rabbi who presided that evening, told us that families and friends, the congregations of temples, are meant to live in these fragile places for seven days, even sleeping there, under stars that seem much nearer than those above our usual roofs.

The shelter was temporary, to remind Jews of their nomadic past and to remind them of the Exodus. Even after they had settled somewhat, enough to farm and eat foods they had planted, still they had to move their flocks from one grazing place to another, still they had to move on. The harvest must have been gathered and eaten and saved and packed for travel. The shelter was meant to remind us of how much a shelter of any kind was a gift, a balm, and this one, a recurring part of the harvest, was something to look forward to when they must have been so weary from constant movement. For me, it had a theological beauty too: their altars, like the Sukkot shelters, were temporary, an invention of nomads who carried not only their harvest food but also their arks and bound holy scrolls, and who set up their tables in remote places.

At the Sukkot ritual, we ate ritual foods and shook the branches of ritual plants: willow, myrtle, date palm, and a citron fruit. A fruit in season. In our McDonald's lives, when food can be had anywhere, this celebration brought to me a deep appreciation for how much a harvest was something waited and hoped for all summer, and then was good enough to eat with impunity, to stuff oneself and lie at rest with your tribe and clan while the food soaked into your hungry body.

Sukkot and Communion are both rituals grounded in the history of those who celebrate them and in the elements of food and community. Sukkot must have been originally a cele-bratory proclamation of survival: "We have enough food, and we are still alive this year." (And the modern Sukkot has even more meaning after the Jewish Holocaust.)

Most rituals are based on old realities, such as the har-vest (Sukkot and Ramadan), the winter feast (which became Christmas for Christians and Hanukkah for Jews). The Christian Pentecost has roots in an old Jewish story of how Moses' words turned into stones and flames and could be understood in any language. The three Abrahamic faiths are intertwined like vines or garden snakes, sharing a nomadic past, myths and stories, fathers and mothers, a family tree.

The establishment of a practice, I think, must be to remind us of those old events, in some visceral, bodily sense, even as our lives are different from our ancestors'. Jews are reminded of survival and pleasure in the ritual of Sukkot. The practice of Communion reminds Christians of a meal and many meals shared by followers of a man who wanted them to see a new kingdom. The practices are "after words," after the events are long in the past, and whatever words attached to them may no longer be accurately recalled. The practice remains to keep us in tune with what the original event pointed toward and so that we can add to its meaning and history.

Certainly, every "afterward" does not follow an experience like the one I had that Christmas Eve. Sometimes, after I take Communion, it's as if I have snacked at a paltry buffet. Not a lot of food there.

But whatever happens during Communion, one of the ways to spend the immediate time afterward, after coming out of the experience, is to sit in silence and let it seep into your cells. I tried that, as I sat in the pew on that Christmas Eve, in the same big room, the same church with the man with the amputated fingers, the woman with a stroke, and the girl with the tongue stud. I sat there and tried not to spend too much time wondering about what had happened but rather to let whatever it was be there in the room with me and everyone else. A large part of my mind was rushing around questioning whether I'd actually had this experience, and a much smaller, more vulnerable part was trying to stay connected to it. And then I realized that to stay connected, I had to be open. That openness, I saw, was both the ticket in and the gift of afterward. It was a tiny opening, like the eyes of the woman paralyzed with a stroke, but it was enough.

Part of "afterward" is letting an experience of the holy seep into your cells so that even when your brain decides it didn't happen or you made it up, you have a cellular memory.

This is part of the reason for establishing a practice, like the practice of taking Communion. One of the first rules I learned when I set out to be a writer was that I had to establish a regular habit of writing. I had to set aside time for putting words on a page. If I sat around and waited for inspiration to strike, I would still be sitting around waiting twenty-five years later.

I set aside the hours between eight and noon every day for writing. Sometimes it goes well; many times it's like making a cup of coffee, tasting it, throwing it out, and making another one. Philip Roth once said he spent his time rewriting sentences. But the point is that my brain is trained to do this five days a week. Like a regular workout, I have to get through resistance to show up, but once I show up, my brain (more or less) gets into the groove. I don't have to relearn the whole thing every morning.

A practice means that you do it often enough that you can build on experience, that your body and your mind know the score. (*Oh, okay, we're taking Communion now.*) A regular practice means that the muscle of your soul is ready to be exercised, like your legs when you run or your arms when you swim. If you let too much time go by between exercise sessions, you know how it's like starting all over again.

A regular practice means that the muscle of your soul is ready to be exercised.

Practicing often also has a good residue, an aftermath. It stays with you long after the actual moment of the practice is finished. The same way you can feel the good oxygen flowing in your blood long after a run, or the deep, relaxing muscle-peace after a swim, you can sometimes feel throughout the day the aftereffects of taking Communion. It builds a foundation for the rest of the day or creates a pool that you can dip into and refresh yourself or that will simply present itself to you when you are not looking.

A small warning: When you have an experience of the infinite during a practice, you can spend a lot of time wanting to return to that great feeling of oneness and end up in what might be called spiritual addiction. You find yourself entering into the practice again and again seeking that same feeling, in the same way a runner seeks a high or an addict seeks that first blast of a drug. This is probably not the point of a practice. (But the desire is not to be condescended to. A friend of mine who had many experiences of God in his youth, so many that he became a priest, said wistfully that he had not had any recently and he missed them.)

One of the ways to counteract the desire to repeat the same feeling again and again is to connect the experiences of a spiritual high, like the one I had that Christmas Eve, with the rest of life. Or at least begin to connect it. This ground is pretty dicey. A deep spiritual event can fall apart under the scrutiny of the rational mind, or it can become weightless and untethered. The Church often doesn't help in this matter because mystical experiences make the Church nervous. Simone Weil, the

French theologian and mystic, called them "events of a different order."[1]

The Church's nervousness is at least partially understandable. Many of us religious persons can climb into an energy that is human-made: emotional, heady, and exciting, contracted through others like a virus, that doesn't really have much to do with God. *Let's get high together!* Or you can get into a kind of mushy "we are all connected," and it feels as if we are all kind of like oatmeal. But while there may be many reasons for having a deep experience of the holy, one of them, it seems to me, is to add to its dimension and our understanding of it.

I could say that my experience that Christmas Eve tells us that there is a lot of movement in God, and a lot of connection. That one aspect of God is like a human dance. This has been said before, and that's interesting too. How are mystical experiences alike? And why? My experience that evening is also like Dr. Taylor's experience of the left side of her brain during her stroke. A full experience of the infinite. Her experience was solitary—that is, she was not with other people when she had it—but she also felt deeply connected to "everything," as she put it.[2] My experience was similar in its rich transcendence to the author Elizabeth Gilbert's description of enlightenment during a long meditation retreat in India, in which she felt as if she had left the planet and was part of the long reach of the universe, but my experience was also different from hers.[3] Why is that?

> *My experience that Christmas Eve tells us that there is*
> *a lot of movement in God, and a lot of connection.*

One of the things I do with this kind of experience is talk about it in our base community, a small group within my church who meet once a week to read the gospel for the next Sunday and reflect on both it and our daily lives. These are people with integrity, with long experience of faith, and who are not easily impressed. We don't sit around wowing each other with our fabulous mystical highs. But we have started to talk about events of a different order with some trepidation and some anxiety, to find out what each other's experiences are like, what characteristics these events have, what they may say about the character and nature of God, and above all, what they point to, what they ask of us.

I wish I could say to you that I now know exactly what that Christmas Eve experience was about. But I cannot. One important thing I know now that I did not know until I had thought and talked about it with my trusted base community is this: it was not only "my" experience. I was part of that Christmas Eve event; I witnessed it.

I felt afterward, as I said, the slightest opening, the beginning of change; and it happened because I was thrown together for one evening with persons unlike myself and ate with them a ritual food that made a bridge between us. Transformation occurs in encounters, sometimes better named collisions, either with the self or with others or with the holy. Jesus was educated and transformed by his encounters, most memorably the one with the Canaanite woman who demanded that he heal her daughter (Matt. 15:21–28). That encounter was a foreshadowing of the kingdom, a glimpse of light.

> *Transformation occurs in encounters, sometimes better named collisions, either with the self or with others or with the holy.*

The Canaanite woman knelt at the feet of Jesus and told him of her need. *Save my daughter from mental illness. Heal her of the demons that haunt her. Restore her as she once was to us.* This woman was stripped down by her need. It's the kind of need that knocks us to our knees. She was willing to beg, willing to risk humiliation. And it would have been complete humiliation. For a Jewish rabbi in first-century Jerusalem to pay any attention to a woman, much less a Gentile woman, was impossible, an outrage. She must have heard something about Jesus' healing powers and felt she had no other alternative. So she arrived at his feet and got exactly the treatment she must have expected.

Jesus, walking through the crowds, suddenly found this Gentile woman at his feet, her hands open, begging him to heal her daughter. His immediate answer was, basically, "I've come for my own people, for Jews, not for you" (v. 24). She replied, "Even the dogs are given crumbs off the table" (v. 27).

He stopped. You can picture the scene. The young rabbi, sure of his call, was suddenly offered a new reality. It came up from the grass, from the rabble at his feet.

He was struck both by her boldness and her need. He was changed by it. In the midst of his own journey, sure of his destiny, he was waylaid by compassion.

"Because of what you said," he told her, "your daughter is healed."

But he, too, was "healed." He was opened. He was changed. He was no longer so sure of what his job was, what he was meant to do. It may be that this is what kept happening to him, over and over again. He met a blind man and was changed by the encounter; he met a woman at a well and Mary Magdalene and a tax collector. The difference between Jesus and us may not merely be one of degrees of divinity, but also his openness to others and their capacity to bend and awaken his heart.

6

EATING THE BODY AND BLOOD

When the wine gave out, the mother of Jesus said to him,
"They have no wine."

—JOHN 2:3

I BEGAN SERVING COMMUNION IN THE WINTER SEVENTEEN years ago. I don't know what, exactly, drew me toward the job. I made an appointment with the priest who was then at Trinity. (Lay Eucharistic Ministers are licensed by the bishop in the Episcopal Church to serve Communion and must be approved by their parish priests.) He told me he would soon teach a class for LEMs. And so I found myself in the parish hall with a few other people, studying handouts and learning how to grip the chalice. What we learned bore no resemblance to what serving Communion was actually like.

The first time I served, I felt as if I were walking on quicksand. I lived in fear of spilling. And once, I served a young man in a nice tan T-shirt and I poured the blood of Christ all down his front. We stared at each other for a second, and then I had to move on. In the sacristy afterward I whispered to a priest, "I spilled wine all over this guy." He paused while wiping off a paten, looked thoughtful, and replied, "That's too bad. I guess we'll have to burn him."

As I served Sunday after Sunday, I stopped being so terrified, but I often felt as if I were in the middle of a collision between the divine and the human. As I grew more used to it, I began to step out of the way. Like a pane of glass, I was the translucent medium through which light passed.

> *As I served Sunday after Sunday, I stopped being so terrified, but I often felt as if I were in the middle of a collision between the divine and the human.*

A bishop I knew, Dan Corrigan, used to call Communion "celebrating the mysteries." He talked about traveling to the Lakota-Sioux reservation in Wisconsin in the twenties to celebrate on a Sunday.

In Wisconsin Dan was serving communion outside once when a flock of geese wobbled over. Dan walked down the line of communicants and then got to the geese. "The Body of Christ," he said, handing each goose a piece of bread.

The wafers are more substantial these days, a thicker form of fish food. Trinity gets hers from the (Roman Catholic) Benedictine Sisters of Perpetual Adoration in Clyde, Missouri.

They make them in two varieties, whole wheat and white, and ship them in plastic bags.

Returning from Communion one Sunday, I curled my tongue against the roof of my mouth and found a bit of wafer left there. I chewed it. The wine still warmed my throat and stomach. I felt a sudden sure sense of having been fed. *It's food,* I thought, *not a metaphor for food.*

I once asked Andrew Colquhoun, a dry-witted Scot, why he had converted from the Presbyterian Church (where he was a minister) to the Episcopal Church, where he is now a priest and brother with the Order of the Holy Cross. He replied, "I was a chaplain, working in a hospital. People were dying, being born, and suffering all over the place. My theology couldn't explain the chaos. I needed the sacrament."

Martin Smith, an Episcopal priest and author, compares the Eucharist to the provisions an army needs when it stops to rest and eat.

The two sacraments in the Anglican Church, the Eucharist and baptism, are concrete—bread, wine, and water. You touch the wafer and the cup. You see both. Communion is meant to be tactile. The sources of this ritual were real bread and real wine, real food, and some churches make their own bread to remind us of that older meal.

Many of us know the story of the wedding feast at Cana, when Jesus is said to have turned water into wine. While a miracle, certainly, I don't think it was so much a magic trick as an act of restoration. The wine was hidden in the water. Jesus, in his profound and steadfast compassion, found that wine and released it so everyone could drink and be revitalized.

In the clear water of our lives lies undiscovered wine. It is our charge, as men and women, as human beings, to commit ourselves to seeking and finding that heady spirit in our sisters and brothers and in ourselves. How to do that is probably different for everyone, but the first step is to know the wine is there.

Consecrating bread and wine for Communion is like that wedding feast: it calls out of these ordinary elements their essential beauty and their life-giving core.

> *Consecrating bread and wine for Communion is like that wedding feast: it calls out of these ordinary elements their essential beauty and their life-giving core.*

What I grew to see as I served Communion was bits of hidden life, something about to emerge, in the people waiting for it. When I served to people on kneelers, I looked down on the halos of balding men, strands of gray showing through dye; and sometimes saw the shy, skittery look in people's eyes. I could see that people were in the midst of being asked for something. The question for me was only how far we wanted to go.

Taking Communion was not, at first, something I liked or understood. When I was eight, my best friend was a girl who lived down the street. Her family was Roman Catholic. Her house was immaculate, with lots of lace doilies and plastic covering the furniture, and a garden that had concrete paths, laid by her father, everywhere. Her father's name was Edwin. He worked, I believe, as a mechanic. He wore overalls. Her mother cooked fabulous Italian food. After church on Sunday, Edwin always bought a large box of doughnuts. You could order what you wanted from him on Saturday night.

My father was a lawyer. My mother did not put plastic on her furniture. Doughnuts were not really a part of our diet. We went to the Congregational church, where I was bored to tears in Sunday school.

One Sunday, Ann invited me to go to church with her. I asked my mother if I could go and she said, with just a moment's hesitation, yes. The moment's hesitation was enough to tell me what I already knew. Roman Catholics were unfamiliar to my mother, different from what and who she knew. Ann's family was, to my family, exotic. It is hard to put myself back into that era, when Roman Catholics were a different clan and a Roman Catholic had never been elected president. My mother, who was not by nature prejudiced and would later vote for John Kennedy (and march for civil rights and insist on being treated by the first African American doctor hired in Albuquerque), did not really know what to do.

Despite that beat of silence, I went. On our way, Ann talked to me about the many things I had to remember, a mini catechism. I could not take Communion, of course; that was obvious. I was not sure what Communion actually was. Even if I had been a practicing Catholic, I would have had to go to "confession." Ann and her brothers and sisters went every Saturday afternoon to tell the priest about their sins. When the priest lifted the Host, I was to tap my heart three times. I remember the sidewalk as we walked, the blocks leading to the church, the hot summer day in New Mexico, and the frightening and thrilling things I was hearing. It was as if we were walking miles and miles to Lourdes as she talked to me, proudly and authoritatively, about sacrifice and blood and sacred hearts, a vast foreign country full of intrigue and secret rules and ways you could fall short.

The sins-and-confession part really stayed with me, as it had clearly stayed with her. I could feel that she was involved in the whole idea of sin, that it had her, and it had me too. I remember feeling as if her words had around them red velvet and darkness and smoke. We put little lace doilies, resembling those on Ann's mother's furniture, on our heads as we arrived at the church, a fairly modern building for New Mexico. It was not an old adobe cathedral but made of some kind of pinkish brick or stone. It may have been where the German and Italian Catholics went to church in New Mexico rather than the cathedral where Hispanic Catholics attended Mass; a divide was there as well.

The statues of the Virgin caught my eye first. Women in pale blue gowns who had visible hearts with swords through them. The Mass was in Latin, which Ann had neglected to mention, and I was really impressed when she responded in Latin. But mainly what I remember feeling was that I was a stranger, witnessing a ceremony with overtones that were frightening to me: a dark church, the weeping Virgins, an archaic language. Then, when it came time for Communion and the Host was lifted up and displayed, I couldn't get the picture of a dead body, Christ's body, out of my mind. And his blood! This seemed to me to be the epitome of what I was seeing all around me, the apotheosis of the whole weird drama. They were going to eat his body and drink his blood! I watched Ann and her family walk together up to the altar rail, which was a very long way from the altar, and kneel like little children there and tip their heads to receive the Host (they did not receive wine in those days) like birds being fed, and of course I wanted to be with them rather than alone and obvious in the pew, but I really didn't want to eat Christ. If this was Communion, it was not for me.

I never went back. I returned to being bored in the Congregational Sunday school and going over on Sunday after church to eat doughnuts at Ann's house, which seemed to suit everyone.

So I was surprised five years later, when I was thirteen and my mother joined the Episcopal Church, to discover that they ate Jesus too.

My mother, who might have been what we now call a

"seeker," found St. John's Episcopal Cathedral and its rector, Kenneth Kadey, and she fell in love. I did too. I tended to love what my mother loved, but I also found something that felt as if it belonged only to me. The Episcopal liturgy was similar to the Catholic liturgy in its form (words, then Communion, then we're out of here), but it was just different enough to attract rather than repel me. I was older, less afraid of the new, and my mother was my companion.

Many children remember their first minister or their first priest with great clarity. Kenneth Kadey was interested in the same things I was interested in: civil rights and Irish poetry. He preached about Martin Luther King Jr. and led marches on the city sidewalks. He loved Jack Kennedy. He took the radical step of allowing women to attend vestry meetings. He designed a beautiful funeral service. He used to stand at the back of the church with the casket and quote John 11:25: "'I am the resurrection, and the life,' saith the Lord, 'and whosoever liveth and believeth in me shall never die,'" and my mother would whisper, "When he says it, I believe it."

I don't recall any catechism at St. John's, although there must have been one. I was baptized and confirmed, the records show, but I remember neither. I do remember Father Kadey standing on a very tall ladder, changing a lightbulb in the sanctuary, and being impressed that he changed the lightbulb himself rather than asking someone to do it for him.

Father Kadey's method of presiding at Communion was

at once simple and solemn. He gave the lifting up of the Host plenty of time. I was moved by his seriousness and his calm. And I was interested in the stories that were read out loud every Sunday: the prodigal son, the woman at the well, the blind beggar. The psalms that cried out against God. The Flood. I felt the beginnings of what would serve me my whole life: that I was fitting myself into a larger story.

In her book *While They Slept: An Inquiry into the Murder of a Family*, Kathryn Harrison described the Gilley family in Medford, Oregon, in which verbal and physical abuse were rampant. Very few books were allowed into the house except for Harlequin romances. In 1984, when Billy Gilley was eighteen, he killed every member of the family except one, the eldest daughter, Jody, who was sixteen. Jody Gilley was upstairs in her bedroom when Billy clubbed their parents and their younger sister to death with an aluminum baseball bat.

Years later, Jody told Kathryn Harrison what she was thinking at that moment:

She tells me she remembers knowing what she knew, and telling herself it was happening in a book. How many books had she read in which terrible things happened, the situation appeared hopeless, the heroine doomed, when somehow, against all odds, she was saved? Now, Jody told herself, she was a character in a book; she was the girl for whom things looked bad—very bad—but turned out all right. In the end, they always did turn out. . . . *How did she escape?* Jody asked herself. *Did the heroine jump out the window?*[1]

Jody's description of how she survived is not to be reduced to any simple formula, but at least part of her story is about the strength and skill of the imagination to fit itself into a story and to use it for its own ends. Her imagination, fed on something as paltry as romances, was up to this task; it led her to see what she might do to save herself. *She was a character in a book.*

For me, the larger narrative of the Christian religion has been a story, a metaphor into which I have fitted my life. *I am a character in this book.* That process began at St. John's Cathedral. And just as Jody probably acquired other books besides Harlequin romances to use in her life's work of creating a self, I, too, grew to see that the Christian story was not the only story for me. But it is a foundational story, the metaphor to which I return again and again.

> *The larger narrative of the Christian religion has been a story, a metaphor into which I have fitted my life. I am a character in this book.*

At St. John's, I did not have the same reaction to Communion as I had at my friend Ann's church. I had a better grasp of metaphor. There was less emphasis on sin in this denomination, and what sin there was, was explained by Kenneth Kadey. He told me that if you were in a quarrel with someone or held something against someone in your heart, you should clean it up as fast as you could before taking Communion; but if you had done what you could do, gone as far as you could go, then to go ahead and take Communion because you'd need it and God wanted you to have it.

In those days, the Episcopal Church was still nervous about Communion. Many churches at that time didn't serve Communion every Sunday. It was only later, after the Book of Common Prayer was reformed in 1979, that it became a weekly event in almost every Episcopal church.

You may have some of the same issues with Communion that I had earlier in my life. Depending on how you grew up, you may have memories of Communions you did not like, or you may not know anything about it, and therefore feel, as I did when I was eight, completely mystified and more than a little turned off. I would urge you to imagine a new story regarding Communion, rather than the one you may have experienced or heard about. And the more I show up at Communion, I see that there is not one Communion; there are many Communions.

7

MAGIC AND THANKSGIVING

I'm too small in the world, yet not small enough
to be simply in your presence, like a thing—
just as it is.

—Rilke, from *The Book of Hours*

Adjacent to the altar in the Sanctuario de Chimayo, a small adobe church in northern New Mexico, a little pit in the ground holds soft, reddish dirt. On the wall near the pit is a handwritten sign that reads, "If you are a stranger, if you are weary from the struggles in life . . ." The eyes of infant Jesuses look down on the dirt with plaster calm. St. Mary Magdalene kneels in prayer with what looks like a theater curtain behind her. On the walls are photos, crutches left behind, and moving testaments to the healing properties of the dirt. It is not unlike a small version of Lourdes. The dirt is supposed to cure pains, rheumatism, sadness, sore throat, paralysis, and is useful during childbirth, reports Stephen F. de Borhegyi, who wrote an expert study of the Sanctuario.[1] You may dissolve the earth in water and drink it or make a paste to place like a poultice on your ailing limbs. One story holds that the dirt when sprinkled on a fire during a lightning storm will cause the weather to calm down.

But the priest in charge of the Sanctuario, the Reverend Casimiro Roca, is frustrated by how much emphasis is placed on the dirt itself. Rev. Roca was recently quoted in the *New York Times* as saying, "It's not the dirt that makes the miracles!"[2]

The dirt is completely ordinary. Roca even has to order clean dirt to be trucked in or the pit would run out. I always tell people that I have no faith in the dirt, I have faith in the Lord," he said in the *Times* story. "But people can believe what they want."[3]

Communion wafers are as ordinary as the dirt at the Sanctuario. They are made by various organizations and religious orders out of perfectly ordinary water and flour. The wine, too, is nothing special. Trinity buys hers at a discount liquor distributor.

We get fixed on the material thing: the holy water, the miraculous dirt, the Communion wafers. I myself have a small amount of Sanctuario dirt in a pot from New Mexico sitting on my bookshelf, carried all the way from New Mexico to California in a baggie. And as I served at the altar one Sunday, a visiting bishop dropped a bunch of wafers on the floor. I (along with a priest) dropped to all fours and began eating them. Throwing them into the garbage was not an option. Yet the line is thin between respectful treatment of certain ceremonial objects and a belief in their magical potency. If we had missed one wafer and it had been vacuumed up, would God have struck us dead? If you answered yes, let's start over.

For many of us, rituals can become not avenues to a deeper understanding of reality or a deepening of faith, but instead a form of magic. *If I eat this wafer, I'll be instantly transformed.*

Rituals may seem to originate in magical thinking: we see the ancient practices of primitive people as methods to hold off or thank the gods, to ward off evil, to suck rain from the dry sky. But these are not to be dismissed as the inventions of ignorant people. Our ancestors were tough and creative; rituals were part of their lives. Knowing there were larger waves of power, meaning, and connection in the world than the ones they could see, they created ways to recognize and inhabit them. While we may condescend to a rain dance, the need to see beyond this world into another one is inherent in that dance; and the need to communicate our deepest desires is there as well. While it is true that we want signs of God's presence that are written in human language, it's the only language we have. And while any ritual can be reduced to magic, just about all of them contain an element of something that is deeply meaningful and human: the element of thanksgiving.

> *While any ritual can be reduced to magic, just about all of them contain an element of something that is deeply meaningful and human: the element of thanksgiving.*

Eucharist in Greek can be translated "thanksgiving." Holy Communion is a way of saying thanks. It points toward abundance. Its lineage may not be so much the Last Supper with its emphasis on sacrifice and death, but more the feeding of the five thousand with its images of abundance and gratitude.

In Proverbs, as Wisdom lays her table for the feast to come, she calls out from her house, "Come, eat of my bread and drink of the wine I have mixed. Lay aside immaturity, and live" (Proverbs 9:5–6). Wisdom prepares a feast and sets her table, and she invites everyone in to sit down and eat.

The movie *Babette's Feast* is the story of two sisters, living alone in a remote coastal village in northern Norway. They are in their middle age, good women. Their idea of a good meal is a piece of salted cod. Their father, a pastor, has died; their church community dwindles and grows gossipy and backstabbing.

Enter into this scene, Babette, a French refugee. She offers to cook for them in exchange for room and board.

For fourteen years, Babette cooks salted cod, ale soup with bread, but with her own special touch. Her only contact with France is a once-a-year splurge: she buys a lottery ticket by mail.

One day a letter arrives for Babette. You guessed it. She's won ten thousand francs, enough to pay her passage home and live on once she arrives. Babette asks her benefactors if she might cook one last meal, a dinner for twelve at her expense.

Cages of quail arrive from France: wines, cheeses, fresh eggs and butter and herbs. The sisters begin to panic: what to do with such extravagance? Such excess?

The day of the feast comes. Babette sets the table with fine linens and candles, crystal and china. And the guests arrive— most of them the bickering churchgoers, and there is also a French general, a former suitor of one of the sisters. Middle-aged and successful, he has put into his ambition all the energy and love he once felt for his beloved.

Their eyes widen as they begin to eat. For some, the sips of champagne are the first of a lifetime. The general exclaims over the quail baked in a pastry shell, the wonderful cheeses. He says, "Surely, this food is exactly like a meal I once had at Chez Angelique, a restaurant in Paris. Its chef was the only woman chef in all of France." As they eat and drink, their smiles begin. For some, it is the first time they've eaten really good food in a whole lifetime of deprivation. Hesitantly, and then with more gusto, they begin to talk. One man opens a sore subject with another: "You cheated me," he says calmly. "Yes, I did," replies the other. "Oh, well," the first man responds. "I cheated you too." And they shake hands. Two women who have gossiped rudely about each other throughout their lives smile warmly at each other and lift their glasses in a toast. And as the coffee and dessert are laid on the table, with more champagne, the general lifts his glass to the whole community.

"Mercy is infinite," he says. "All that we need is given to us."

Then he adds, "And even what we have rejected in our lives," he says, looking at the woman he loved long ago, "will, in the end, be granted to us."

At the end of the film, we discover that Babette, of course, was the chef at Chez Angelique, but the greater surprise is she is not leaving after all. Why not? Because a meal for twelve at Chez Angelique costs ten thousand francs. Babette has given them everything. And this may be the final reason the dinner was so transforming: it was given with complete generosity, with nothing held back. Babette knew how to say thanks.

Babette's Feast is a story about the healing powers of extravagance, of extravagant generosity, of extravagant love. This is the feast that Wisdom invites us to eat. Do we know how to eat it? Or do we settle for crusts and salted cod? Are we like the people the archbishop of Canterbury talked about in a recent sermon, who understand everything about bread except that you are meant to eat it?

A story from my life might illustrate this dilemma. Several years ago, my former mother-in-law, the mother of my first husband, was dying in Palo Alto, California. When I heard she was near death, I wrote her a letter about what she had meant to me when I was eighteen years old, married and far too young. I told her she had given me a sane model for a mother, a person who was consistent, loving, and helpful. I said that the essence of healing is that when someone is committed to helping and understanding us, we can make the chaotic and traumatic events of our lives into a new story, a new life. Betty Stern, I said, helped me rewrite my life.

The day after she died, my former brother-in-law called to ask me to come to her funeral and speak, to say the things I'd said in the letter. I was stunned. This family had been beloved to me, but I had not seen some of them in almost twenty years. I had many excuses at the ready, and I was really scared, but my former brother-in-law was crying, and I said yes. I flew up to Palo Alto from Santa Barbara for the day and spoke at Betty's funeral, and I saw this family and their friends again. We did what families do when they reunite, as if the time that had passed had been the blink of an eye: we looked at photographs of Betty and her husband, John; we told stories about her brilliant mind, her wit, and her famously beautiful shoes. We cried and we laughed, and we caught up with each other. We made in our grief, acts of love. When John Stern introduced me to a friend, he said, "Well, Nora is . . . Nora is my daughter."

After I was divorced, in my early twenties, it was important to separate from this family, so influential on one so young. But later, as I grew older, there was no need for the separation. Yet I continued not to see them. There were good reasons: I had a new marriage; I was busy; my own family had its own rich treasures. And yet, I think I was like those sisters in *Babette's Feast* who denied themselves food and ate salted cod. That family was in the past, I told myself, if I said anything to myself at all, and I couldn't have them in my life again. I learned at Betty

Stern's funeral that that was not true: because mercy is infinite, and even what we reject is returned to us.

I want to place two worlds in front of you today: one is the world of propriety, rules, and regulations, what is done and what is not done, lines that are drawn to keep people out. It's a world where it is inappropriate for a former daughter-in-law to speak at her former mother-in-law's funeral. Inappropriate for someone's cook to spend all her money on a farewell feast. It's a world of sticking to principles. It's got plenty of stuff in it: lots to buy, lots to envy, but not much real food. Let's call this world one of crusts and salted cod and stale loaves.

Now I'd like us to imagine it as a little tableau, like a Brueghel painting: There is my former brother-in-law sitting beside the telephone. There I am, just before I answer it. Moments before an invitation is offered, before a choice is made.

The events in this story could have turned out differently, for perfectly satisfactory reasons. My former brother-in-law could have decided it was just too awkward. I could have said to him when he called that my calendar was just too full.

And yet it was not so. Instead, each one of us was given the grace to move outside the world as it is, and into another place. We took a risk, accepted an invitation; we smelled the scent of fresh, baking bread. We were given the grace to leave behind our small lives, our drawn lines, our starvation diets, our immaturity, to feast at that heavenly banquet prepared for us at the foundations of the world.

The place of extravagant food is hidden, undeniably fragile, and full of risk and heartbreak. Yet Jesus bets everything on this world. He sets it above principalities and powers. Above custom, practice, taboo, and theory. Above canons of the church, above the opinion of your neighbors. It is the place where mercy is infinite, where all that we need is given to us, and even what we have rejected is returned to us. It is the kingdom of living bread.

We are meant to eat of this bread, to sit down at this feast. When we as a people live for that bread and cast our lot with it, we create nothing less than the kingdom for which Jesus gave his life. It is all around us, all the time, this beautiful world, just about to happen.

> *When we as a people live for that bread and cast our lot with it, we create nothing less than the kingdom for which Jesus gave his life.*

The Communion ritual is a way of putting aside time to give our thanks—and in that putting aside of time, we have the opportunity to see what our lives are like now and what they can become. We might see, as I did in the story of my former mother-in-law, what gifts have been lying around unopened. The old dances and practices performed by our ancestors may have been a way of saying thanks for the gifts that had come their way already, rather than a manipulative method to get more of them. (Or, in some hands, they may have been both.)

We, too, may come to Communion with twin desires: to give

thanks and to seek a magical solution to a given problem. I see nothing wrong in the desire for magic; it's who we are. To admit that I want and need a wand passed over my immediate trouble, is honest and wise. But I have to know, in the end, that the world is complex, with layers of meaning and coherence, and that the Communion wafer is not a wand; it is instead a compass. It points outward, toward the vast ocean outside my small self, that my small self is also made of and knows. It points to what has been and what can be but also opens your eyes to what is right now. This will put you in the role of prophet. Prophecy, as the conservation biologist David Ehrenfeld said about George Orwell, is not about foretelling the future, but is about describing the present with exceptional truthfulness and accuracy.[4]

The wafer and wine are no more magic potions than is the dirt at the Sanctuario in New Mexico, but they partake of the same quality. They are concrete things that stand in for something invisible and mute, recognized by human minds as avenues into the sacred. Who knows how the hole in the ground in Chimayo became a holy place? The stories of its origin say it was once a hot spring. Tewa Native Americans, who predate the Spanish in the valley, call the dirt "blessed." Someone may have seen into the deep there and told a story about it. A woman who smoothed the earth on her hips might have felt alive again. Many people followed and repeated their own stories. The dirt is just dirt, and the wafer is just a wafer, but they are sanctified by human feet and hands, and human stories. They have specific histories, like road maps, that set them apart from ordinary life, yet they are made of the most ordinary things. In this sense, the dirt and the wafer join the ordinary world to the extraordinary, knitting them together with filament as fine as a spider's web. In the act of eating the wafer or using the dirt, we open ourselves, our hearts and minds, to the place where there is no time and where everything is being remade and reborn, a mystery of recreation and reconstruction.

We need concrete things that tie the ordinary to the extraordinary, like the long lines that tether a hot air balloon to the ground, to bring the kingdom of heaven near to us. The hope is that these rituals will not diminish the holy nor make it mundane but are set aside to keep it close.

8

MYTHS AND TRADITIONS

"I CAN'T TAKE COMMUNION BECAUSE I AM MAD AT SOMEONE."

"I can't take Communion because I am still drinking and can't stop."

"I can't take Communion because I screamed at my husband this morning."

"I can't take Communion because I stole a CD yesterday."

"I can't take Communion because I had breakfast this morning."

Communion has many myths and traditions attached to it. People are often confused about what holds true in a given church and what is a tradition from the past that is no longer viable.

Here is a question often asked about Communion: Is it really the body of Christ? And what about the blood? Do the bread and wine literally turn into the physical body and blood of Christ?

No, and yes. No, the bread from the Sisters of Mercy from Clyde, Missouri, doesn't turn into flesh and bones. No, the wine the church buys from a local liquor distributor doesn't magically turn into type O blood when the priest sweeps his hand over it. But yes, in another way. The writer Flannery O'Connor, a Catholic, said, "If it's a symbol, then to hell with it."[1]

How often should you take Communion? Can you take it if you doubt parts of the Christian story? If you are divorced? What if you are not baptized?

Certainly, it makes sense to have some kind of relationship to the Christian story in order to take Communion. But if your concern comes from old associations or teachings and is about being in exactly the right place to take Communion, then I urge you to think again.

> *If your concern comes from old associations or teachings and is about being in exactly the right place to take Communion, then I urge you to think again.*

It is traditional in some churches that persons who take Communion have to be baptized. Baptism is complex and multilayered, but it is about signing on, in an outward and visible way, to the Christian story. Communion is so important to me that I don't think there should be rules about who can take it and who cannot. I am going to make a strong case for my point of view, but please understand that I respect other traditions regarding this sacred ritual.

It's wise to find out what your church's rules are regarding Communion before jumping up to join everyone at the altar. Our church makes it very clear: wherever you are in your journey of faith, our priests say, you are welcome at Communion.

My own view is this: that once you decide that there are rules around who takes Communion and who doesn't, you can get to the point where taking Communion boils down to making sure a soul is freshly laundered and squeaky-clean before its body can take the bread and wine into its mouth. This gets very close to manipulating God. And once you begin to make rules, then there is no end to the rule making.

> *Once you begin to make rules, then there*
> *is no end to the rule making.*

When I worked in a soup kitchen in Trinity's parish hall, we learned this lesson well. When we first opened the kitchen, we were told we should have a monitor at the door who would interview people as to whether or not they were in shape to come inside. We were to make a list of rules about who we served and who we did not allow to come in. But once we started thinking about it, we realized that the idea of a monitor and rules ran against the grain of what we were trying to do in the soup kitchen. We wanted to feed people. So we decided to follow another model and have no rules and no monitor and wait to see what happened. Gradually, over time, the men and women we served in the kitchen asked us to make one rule: if someone was obnoxious, he or she had to go outside. That was it. In the five years of the soup kitchen's life at Trinity, we had no serious incidents. Once, a man threw his tray down in front of the soup line when I happened to be serving. I asked him if he was asking me to call the police, and he said yes. So I did.

We understood that once you begin to make rules in a soup kitchen or in a lot of other places, you never stop. I once visited a soup kitchen where the rules were posted on a board near the entrance. There were about thirty rules, including this one: you could not have sexual intercourse within thirty feet of the building. I wondered how they had arrived at thirty feet.

If you make up a bunch of rules about who gets to take Communion and who doesn't, then Communion is reduced either to a special club with only certain kinds of people who are allowed in, or magic: "If I have confessed my sins, then something wonderful will happen. If I have not, then it won't."

> *If you make up a bunch of rules about who gets to take Communion and who doesn't, then Communion is reduced either to a special club with only certain kinds of people who are allowed in, or magic.*

A friend, Anne Howard, tells a story about visiting the cathedral at Durham in the United Kingdom, to see the shrine of

St. Cuthbert, the seventh-century monk famous for his healing powers. Anne and her husband and son entered the cathedral, pulling open the huge, heavy door with a huge brass lion's head door knocker. She was not ready for what was inside . . . "Massive columns of stone carved eight hundred years ago rose up around me," Anne said. "A mighty fortress indeed. The whole place spoke of power, frankly, the power and might of Norman kings more than the holiness of God.

"And then I looked down at the floor and saw a long, wide black marble line inlaid in the stone floor. It stretched across the entire width of the nave, across the back end, the west end. I had never seen anything like it. And then I looked up and saw a framed sign posted on the column, explaining the line. The sign said the marble was laid there in the 1100s when the cathedral was built to keep the women back, to keep the women away from the main part of the church. It was a protective barrier, to keep the altar and St. Cuthbert's holy shrine pure and free from the corrupting power of women.

"It hurt to see that line," Anne said. "It hurts to remember it even now—that barrier established in the name of purity."

No more than God meant there to be a line preserving St. Cuthbert's shrine from women do I believe that God means there to be a line that separates you and me from taking Communion.

It was risky not to have any rules at our soup kitchen in Trinity's parish hall. Social workers would come to visit their clients there, and one of them once said, "Do you know who you have seated here today? I mean, you've got prostitutes and drug—" I held up my hand.

"I don't want to know," I said.

Everyone was welcome at the soup kitchen. It was not up to us to ask questions and be the judges of who should be fed. And this is true for Communion as well. Jesus practiced a radical faith: everyone was welcome at his table.

Jesus practiced a radical faith: everyone was welcome at his table.

You are welcome at this table. The altar is the big table. This is the table that wants everyone there: poor and rich, women and men, children and older people, the mentally disabled and depressed, the homeless, the sane, the happy and the sad, the straight and the gay and the in-between. Thieves are welcome here, and embezzlers; so are murderers and prostitutes and sex abusers and those who have been or are abused. Those who have had abortions are welcome here as well as those who have not. Drinking alcoholics, and those who've joined AA or have quit. Everyone. Just like the tax collectors and the blind man and the leper who followed Jesus. The gospel story that makes the most sense to me about the Eucharist is the feeding of the five thousand. Jesus didn't ask those thousands of people camped on that hillside whether they had confessed their sins or how clean they were. He fed them.

But if everyone is welcome, in whatever state you happen to

be, is there anything to do to prepare for taking Communion? I speak for myself, but this is what I try to do. I try to bring my whole self to the table. All the good stuff and the bad. Everything. Empathy. Compassion. Fortitude. Courage. Selfishness. Fear. Defensiveness. The part of me that lies. The part that envies. The wife who screams at my husband. The woman who doesn't speak to her neighbor on the street. The one who doesn't give enough to the poor and wants more clothes. The part that wants to be famous and doesn't listen. The part that is a good friend to many friends. The part that loves my godchildren. The part that doesn't address or protest the very things that meant so much to Jesus: the domination of empire, the ruling elite, systemic corruption.

I hope, not to become one with God in such a way as to lose my own sense of self and boundaries, but instead to become in God more like myself. "Like a night sky in the Greek poem, I see with a myriad eyes, but it is still I who see," said C. S. Lewis. "Here, as in worship, in love, in moral action, and in knowing, I transcend myself; and am never more myself than when I do."[2]

Each one of us is unique. There is no one like you anywhere in the world, and there will never be again another person like you. Bring yourself to the table.

You are a guest at God's feast. You are an honored guest. You are a friend here. You are loved the way a friend is loved. Your best friend knows your flaws and foibles but loves you nevertheless.

You are a guest at God's feast. You are an honored guest.

If Jesus were here, and he is, he would wash your feet. Remember, that's what he did at the very end of his life. He honored his friends.

The point is not to dishonor God by refusing the banquet. The point is to feed yourself so you can have strength, courage, fortitude, empathy, generosity, all of those things that are in short supply in the world.

And to open yourself. I once served Communion to a man I knew only slightly who really looked at me in the eyes when I served him and allowed his vulnerability to show, and I was given the courage to do the same thing back. Imagine, if we did that for each other on the street.

Do the bread and wine literally turn into the physical body and blood of Christ?

The bread from the Sisters of Mercy from Clyde, Missouri, doesn't turn into flesh and bones. The wine the church buys from a local liquor distributor doesn't magically turn into type O blood.

It's something else. Holy Communion is an act of the imagination.

Imagination has something of a bad rap these days: memoir sells better than fiction. But imagination is a peculiar and singular human gift. To take bread and wine in this peculiar way invites you to imagine your way into some other place. Our imaginations reach out toward that other world, and that other world may draw close. It's a way to leap into the infinite, to be met there by something else, a Being who communicates in unseen ways. Our imaginations may be the closest things we have to God's language. And Communion speaks to and opens our imaginations; it's one of the places where our imaginations are primed and fed.

Taking Communion every Sunday is a creative act, and it makes no more "sense" than writing a poem, or, for that matter, reading one. It isn't going to get you anywhere in the world; it's not networking; it has no practical worth. Every creative act, Simone Weil said, is a "folly of love."[3]

Taking Communion every Sunday is a creative act.

In the novel *The Violent Bear It Away*, Flannery O'Connor wrote about a crowd of people who are fed on a hill. In the novel gradually you see that this gathering of people on a hillside is the same as the one in the loaves and the fishes, the parable of Jesus feeding the five thousand:

> The old man was lowering himself to the ground and when
> he was down and his bulk was settled, he leaned forward,
> toward the basket, impatiently following its progress toward

him. The boy too leaned forward, aware at last of the object of his hunger, aware that it was the same as the old man's and that nothing on earth would fill him. His hunger was so great that he would have eaten all of the loaves and fishes after they were multiplied.[4]

I find this kind of imagery much more helpful to me when contemplating Communion than lots of rules and regulations about who can take it and who cannot or whether we believe that it's the real body and the real blood. The old man and the boy are hungry for something that can't easily be satisfied. They lean forward impatiently for the basket coming their way.

If you are hungry for Communion, take it.

9

A HISTORY IN BRIEF

There are hundreds of ways to kiss the ground.

—RUMI

ONE YEAR, I WAS INVITED BY A RABBI TO A PASSOVER SEDER held at our local temple. In her introductory remarks, the rabbi said this was the evening when "we eat our history." She meant that the symbolic food eaten at a Seder, of which there are many—an egg, bitter herbs, matzo bread—stand for historical events in Judaism. The bitter herbs, including parsley dipped in salt water and eaten, symbolize the bitter tears the Israelites shed when they left slavery in Egypt for an unknown fate. The bread is unleavened bread because the Israelites didn't have a chance to wait for their bread to rise before leaving their homes forever. And at this Seder, we removed ten drops of wine from each of our cups, with the tips of our fingers or with a spoon, and placed them on our plates, to symbolize the ten plagues that God rained on Egypt to punish her leaders for their abuse of their slaves and to remember, the rabbi said, that everywhere people are suffering. The drops of wine looked like pale drops of blood.

In Islam, there is the practice of fasting during Ramadan, which takes place every year in the autumn months. From sunrise to sunset, only water is taken for thirty days. After sunset, a meal is eaten. And at the very end of Ramadan, a big meal is eaten. I attended one of those suppers, at the end of the season, at a large interfaith gathering here in Santa Barbara at a local Presbyterian church. We were all kind of awkward as we walked in: Jews, Muslims, Christians, all of us descendants of the same Abraham as our religious father, and now separate, wary, and in some parts of the world, at war. Women with head scarves worked busily over platters of food. Young men with their heads wrapped in cloth sat together at tables, getting ready for the prayers to be said at sunset. The rest of us tried to find our place names at circular tables.

Excitement filled the room as the exact hour of the sun's setting came near. I saw how lovely it was to really mark the setting of the sun, not as something that just happened, that we hardly notice (unless we are out hiking too late or our children are still playing outside), but as an important event, a big transition.

It was announced that the Muslim men and women would be gathering in a separate room to say their prayers before we sat down to the meal. I asked if I could go into the room with them, to watch. Someone said, "Of course; just remember to take off your shoes."

I intended just to witness Muslim prayers, having only seen them once in Washington, D.C., at a large mosque and only then while passing by in a car. But the room was small, and I found myself, not in the far back, as I had intended, but in one of the lines of women toward the middle. Pretty soon, I found myself doing exactly what the woman sitting next to me was doing. That is, standing up, falling to my knees, leaning forward and pressing my forehead to the floor, rising to my knees, and then repeating it. It was amazing. It was the most bodily prayer I have ever experienced. The closest thing I had done to it was during yoga, in child's pose, in which you sit on your feet and then press your head to the floor, and I wondered how these two might have been intertwined at some time, ages ago.

Then we got up and filed back into the dining room, where we ate the fabulous *Iftar* meal, the meal to break the fast, starting with dates, and then working our way through lamb and chicken, various delicious rice dishes, and red peppers with slivers of onion. We talked with people we had never met who practiced a religion most of us had only heard about in newspaper headlines.

Each of our three traditions flows from Abraham. The foundational story for a meal is in Genesis 18, the story of Abraham's welcome of three strangers who arrive at his tent in the desert. He offers them not only food but a feast. The strangers turn out to be angels who bless Abraham and his wife, Sarah, after his generous meal and make him a new father, a new person, and the founder of a new nation. A stranger can be treated in two ways, it seems to me: one is as the enemy, and the other is as a new opportunity, a gift of newness. The stranger offers us a new way of looking at things, and in return, the stranger sees our way of doing things as new to him or her. I was a stranger at this interfaith gathering, and I was welcomed. I came away energized by a new way of praying and well fed.

Food, because it is so basic to us, has long been central to ritual and worship. Ancient people often sacrificed or made offerings of food to their gods. They built special tables for these offerings that became altars. Even today, many world religions still include food in their rituals. Writes Helen Volz, a minister, "The Shintoists offer fruit and vegetables to the Kami; Buddhists put a bowl of rice before the statue of Gautama. Sikhs share a special pudding in their temples; Jews ask God to bless bread and wine on Friday night."[1]

When a friend of mine who is a priest showed off his newly furbished church to a young Japanese woman who had never seen a Christian church, she took one look at the altar and said, "Oh, you have a meal here."

Within Communion, and even in the way we still practice it, are its Jewish roots. Jesus, as many Christians forget, was a Jew. He came not to create a new religion but to revive and restore an old one.

Some scholars believe that the roots of the Eucharist lie in

Jewish liturgies. The first half of the Christian Eucharistic liturgy may come from the Jewish Sabbath morning service and the second half from the Passover meal or Seder. Other scholars think the Eucharist was derived not from the Seder but from the regular Jewish evening meal that inaugurated the Sabbath and festivals; the Eucharistic prayer evolved out of the grace said on those occasions.

The Strasbourg papyrus is a fragment from a document probably written in the fourth or fifth century, but it may be older. In fact, it may be the oldest Eucharist prayer yet found. It looks as if it was meant to be complete prayer. There is nothing specific in it about blessing a meal; instead it's a thanksgiving prayer with structure: thanks, offering, intercessions. It also mentions a kind of sacrifice, not a bodily sacrifice but a symbolic one, with incense as an offering, and it mentions a reasonable sacrifice and bloodless worship.

It's traditonal to think that the shape of Communion or the Eucharist (taking bread and wine, saying thanks, breaking the bread, and then sharing bread and wine) comes from Jesus' words and actions at the Last Supper. But Paul Bradshaw, an authority on the Eucharist, says it's more accurate to say its roots are in the *various* meals that Jesus shared with his followers and others throughout his life. Bradshaw also notes that each early Christian community seems to have had its own form of communal meal practice; a standard form emerged much later. "Some gatherings of early Christians practiced a meal in which the cup ritual seems to have preceded rather than followed the bread ritual," Bradshaw wrote. "Others linked themselves to the Last Supper."[2]

The early Christians practiced some form of an early Communion ritual, and in each house, it was probably different. As well as the cup and wine ritual, these early communities almost always had a meal together. In other words, the ritual was linked to actual food, a real meal, a gathering of friends over dinner. Only later were meal and Eucharist separated.

Justin Martyr, a second-century Christian and one of the earliest sources of information about the early church, described public gatherings in Rome: "On the day called Sunday all who live in cities or in the country gather together in one place . . . and when our prayer is ended, bread and wine and water are brought, and the president in like manner offers prayers and thanksgivings, according to his ability."[3] But Paul Bradshaw cautions us against concluding that this is what went on *everywhere*. "There is no justification at all, for concluding that what these authors describe as practices familiar in their region were necessarily the universal customs of the time."[4]

I like to think of those early Communions as folding a sacred version of bread and wine inside ordinary bread and wine, the way the feeling of having a soul, a self, in touch with something wider and deeper, is inside the skin and mind, inside our everyday selves. I love the idea of the two together, the meal and the holy meal, a binding of sacred and secular, the ordinary and the extraordinary, so that the two don't end up separated into realms that don't ever speak to each other.

The closest to the early house church meal I've seen is on Maundy Thursday at my church when we gather for dinner and in the midst of it have Communion. Recently I arrived early to the parish hall where the dinner was served. Volunteers had put tables end to end and covered them with white ironed cloths or sheets. A whole crew had made centerpieces of lambs' ears and spring bulbs. Bottles of wine (Trader Joe's bargains) began to appear. After we sat down, one of the laypeople at my table welcomed the 150 people who were there and led a short prayer. And we set to eating salad, drinking wine, and chatting as we would at any dinner. I asked a friend sitting next to me how her middle daughter was doing in school. A woman I knew only slightly asked me where I had bought my shoes.

In the midst of this, we washed each other's feet, at several stations around the room. My friend Ann and I were attendants at one station: it was our responsibility to make sure there was enough water and enough clean towels, and to dump the used water. Each table came as a group, and by pairs, they washed each other's feet, one person on a small stool and the other in a chair. Our minister asked people to think about what they were most concerned about, what weighed on them, and then perhaps to voice it to the person who was washing his or her feet. I didn't know if this would work; I was skeptical. The first table got up and walked over, about six people. A woman sat on the stool. A man, a local lawyer, sat in the chair. He took off one of his shoes and his sock, and placed his foot in the plastic tub. I wondered, briefly, how Jesus had washed the feet of his friends (in warm water? in cold water? where did the water come from?). Then the lawyer leaned forward, and as the woman poured water over his foot, he whispered something I could not hear. She listened intently. When they were finished, and he had put his shoe back on, he stood up and she hugged him. It was intimate. The foot washing had created intimacy in the midst of a dinner party. I saw Jesus again as the person who knew how to bring us back to our senses. He did this through simple and profound acts, which we now have made into rituals.

> *I saw Jesus again as the person who knew*
> *how to bring us back to our senses.*

And so to Communion. Right after the soup, one of the priests stood up and started the prayers. "Lift up your hearts," she said, and we replied, "We lift them up unto the Lord."

I was sitting right across the table from her. When we served Communion, we gave it to each other. This, too, was intimate. "The body of Christ," I said to Ann. "The bread of heaven."

"The blood of Christ," the fellow sitting next to me said. "The cup of salvation."

And then, seconds later, I was sipping from my own wine glass again, and we were talking about the presidential primaries.

It must have been something like this, in those early churches. You had the *blessed* meal and the *meal* meal. You were dependent on each other not only for worship but for food. You had sacred life and ordinary life, folded together like a sandwich.

In the fourth century, the Roman emperor Constantine made Christianity the religion of the state—and everything changed. "Celebrated now in large public buildings the Eucharist took on the style of an imperial court ceremony and . . . features drawn from the pagan religions around, of which it saw itself as the true fulfillment," wrote Paul Bradshaw. "Fixed prayers with elevated language began to replace the simpler extemporaneous compositions of earlier times and these together with music, processions and vesture were used to enhance the solemnity of the rite in the eye and ears of the worshippers."[5]

Everything changed. Christianity was transformed from a house-centered gathering of people who shared everything they had to what Bradshaw calls a "favored cult of the Roman empire."[6]

We live with this legacy. Scholars have been and are hard at work, trying to separate out what the Church became after the fourth century from what may have been the original intention of Jesus and his early followers.

Skip ahead from the fourth century to the sixteenth, when Protestants parted from Rome during the Reformation. The Protestants largely abhorred the Eucharist; they considered it to be "Popish." The newly formed Anglican Church in England, however, found the Eucharist central not only to worship but to faith. Elizabethan reformers changed the celebration of the Eucharist from a once-a-year event for the laity (common in the medieval Roman church) to a weekly Communion of the people. The sacraments are not meant to be "gazed upon or to be carried about," wrote the reformers, but "that we should duly use them."[7] At the same time, the Elizabethans disposed of the arguments over transubstantiation—whether the bread and wine changed under the priest's consecration to the actual body and blood of Christ—by stating flatly that the manner in which Christ's presence was in the bread and wine was best left to God.

We're now in the middle of yet another "reformation," says church historian Phyllis Tickle.[8] Tickle says we seem to go through one every five hundred years. This time around, many churches are trying to reclaim the sensibility, at least, of those older, first- and second-century Eucharists. My own church has smaller, more informal Communion gatherings during the week. Lately, we've added a short Communion celebration at the end of our base community–style Bible study. At the very end of our time together, only an hour, we pass consecrated bread and wine to each other around the table, using the very short service for taking Communion to people at home. In this way, I think, we are contributing to the new reformation, by introducing a new way of celebrating Communion, connecting it to our own lives in a direct, intimate setting.

Writes Kenan Osborne, "Each actual sacramental celebration is . . . unique and unrepeatable. The search for an essence of the Eucharist is in this view, meaningless. There are in actuality only a diverse multiplicity of Eucharistic celebrations, each involving individual communities, individual persons, individual co-ordinates of space and time. In these actual celebrations, the divine enters into a deepening relationship with the Christian and each Christian responds in his or her unique way to the blessing of divine presence."[9]

Amen.

10

THE SOUP KITCHEN

Day by day, as they spent much time together in the temple, they broke bread at home and ate their food with glad and generous hearts, praising God and having the goodwill of all the people.

—ACTS 2:46–47

Many of us are asking, "How should I live? How should we live?" We come to our faith communities with those questions. Sometimes they are taken seriously, even answered, and sometimes the church sticks us on a committee.

One of the things that happened to me after I went to church for many years, asking those questions, was I began to see that if you don't act on what you hear in the Gospels every Sunday, then it doesn't stick.

When I first went back to the Episcopal Church after a long hiatus, I loved the ritual. I loved the liturgy of the Episcopal Church: each week, the same form, from the Book of Common Prayer.

The trouble was, I had trouble connecting it back to my

daily life. Church was like a play or a nice concert. I went to the "theater" on Sunday, felt uplifted or moved, but couldn't figure out how to integrate those feelings into my own experience; so gradually they faded as the week wore on. It didn't connect. I suspect that many people who faithfully attend church remain in such a state and don't really know what to do about it. What I finally understood was that simply going to church doesn't do it, but neither does not going to church.

In the last fifteen years, a renewal of interest in the "historical Jesus" has resulted in books, papers, and arguments as to who this person really was. We have known for some time that the Gospels were written long after the death of Jesus and were compiled by men who lived long after him, from stories and scraps of history. Each of these men also had his own point of view and philosophy. Scholars today work to find something of the man behind these stories, to sift out some of his real words and actions, through painstaking examination of the Gospels and comparisons between them and other recently discovered documents.

Certainly, scholars agree that Jesus traveled from town to town, healing and preaching, and lived an itinerant's life. He lived under the Roman Empire and was certainly aware of it. Jesus lived in occupied territory. Israel, Jerusalem, and Galilee were colonized by that great empire: builder of aqueducts, commander of the largest and most efficient army in the world, and inventor of that peculiar form of execution, one they saved for dangerous political terrorists, persons who were threats to the empire itself, charismatic leaders who attracted followers— crucifixion, the cross.

Scholars have studied Jesus' relation to Rome, and for them, neither the term *political activist* nor *personal savior* quite cuts it, but rather something or someone in between.

This ground is delicate: these days, we often make Jesus into only a personal Savior. I don't want to swing all the way the other way and make him into a political revolutionary. That limits him too. But to remove Jesus from his political and historic reality is to deny him, and us, his full story.

Trying to understand Jesus without knowing how Roman imperialism determined the conditions of life in Galilee and Jerusalem would be like trying to understand Martin Luther King Jr. without knowing how slavery, reconstruction, and segregation determined the lives of African Americans in the United States.

But, like King, Jesus did not provoke the empire by armed revolutionary activity. He may have provoked it by insisting that violence, the very underpinning of the empire, would never bring the kingdom of heaven to earth. This, as I said earlier, is a kind of criticism. Having compassion for people who are hurt by an empire becomes a way of criticizing the empire itself. As I also mentioned earlier, Jesus said it is not normal for someone who is blind or deaf to beg on the street.

One of the many radical things Jesus did was to sit down

and eat with people who were the lowest on the rungs of his society. He loved an open table.

> *One of the many radical things Jesus did was to sit down and eat with people who were the lowest on the rungs of his society. He loved an open table.*

Some of the religious leaders of first-century Jerusalem lived by a purity code that not only classified food and habits but classified people into rigid categories, such as "sinners, untouchables, outcasts." People who were sick or maimed were not "whole," and therefore not "pure." Sound familiar? Jesus refused to live this way.

I began to understand both my own faith and what Jesus was up to when I went to work in a soup kitchen.

It started in the base community at Trinity. Modeled after the Latin American *communidades de base*, Trinity's communities work from the same premise as do those in Latin America—that the gospel is a living document, speaking to us aloud, shaking us up. Our community at Trinity had between ten and twelve members. Each week, we'd "check in" by talking about how our prayers have gone that week and then read the gospel for the following Sunday. Then we'd ask ourselves, what is this saying to us in our lives right now? What is it asking us to do?

In the base community, we read the words in Matthew 25:35—"I was hungry and you gave me food"—enough times and talked about it so much that it became impossible not to act one day when the vestry struggled to decide what to do with so many homeless people coming to the office window, begging for food.

"I could go down the street and find out if Vons would give us their old vegetables for soup," Ann Jaqua said one night at the base community.

For the first five months of that kitchen's life, we handed the soup through a little window cut into the back door of the parish hall. The men stood in line outside. Then, it started to rain. The men stood in line outside, drenched and cold, while we stood inside, warm and dry. Finally, we let them in once. Everyone behaved. In fact, they were too well behaved. Almost no one spoke. Tables of silent men filled the hall. They ate and left. After that, it seemed silly not to just let them in. And so for months they sat at the tables, and we stood behind the serving table, grabbing a bite to eat ourselves either at home or in the church's kitchen. Then one day, I noticed that at a table with four men in various states of homelessness, was a well-dressed woman, eating the same food. She was, I realized, a volunteer from another church. The next week, I tried it.

I sat down with a bunch of guys who slowly looked up and greeted me. As I did this week after week, I began to learn their names. Greg, who had mental illness and liked to tell jokes; Alan, a Vietnam vet who watched PBS and ended up volunteering to clean up the dining hall every day, without fail. Other men who drifted in and out of despair and poverty.

I began to understand what Jesus had done when he sat down with outcasts. For an hour, I became an outcast myself. In comparison with religious codes, this was a minimal practice. Religious or social codes are elaborate, divisive, and hierarchical; this was simple, a kind of nothing, but it greatly affected my sense of how the gospels connected to my life. I was "doing" the gospels.

After I'd eaten at the tables with the men and women for a couple of months, when I walked in the door, I felt I was walking toward the same place I sought when I took Communion. And one day, as I handed a guy a bowl of soup, I imagined a river of free vegetables flowing into the kitchen. Our job was to catch the vegetables, make them into soup, and then pass them along. I thought about how weird it would be to charge for the soup: what was freely given had to be freely given away. This was God's economy, I realized. I called it "the economy of abundance."

> *When I walked in the door, I felt I was walking toward the same place I sought when I took Communion.*

The economy of abundance was tenuous: you could not buy your way out of it. We had to rely on what was given to us; cubes of frozen cheese, a box of frozen ham, a gallon of ranch salad dressing were causes for celebration.

In the economy of abundance, you had to scrounge. We begged bread from local bakeries; from butchers who donated meat, we even used the chicken bones left after most of the breast meat was removed; from traveling executives, we were given the soaps and shampoos collected in hotels. On the bottom rungs, I saw that scrounging is a craft. The men we served in the kitchen sifted through wastebaskets at the end of the day and found things I would have missed: hairpins, a half-smoked cigarette, two paper clips. Everything was useful; nothing was wasted. I came to believe God scrounges too. A pregnant, unmarried woman; tax collectors; blind beggars; a son conceived out of wedlock. God uses what is useless, what is discarded, what is low.

We gradually stopped worrying too much about fund-raising, kept our expenses low, and waited to see what would happen next. It felt wild and free.

It did not last in my daily life, always. I'd get on an airplane, be upgraded, and immediately feel contemptuous toward those in economy. But when I recited the Nicene Creed on Sunday morning, the "unseen" became for me, not a realm of ghosts, but a place where you waited and hoped. It was like the soup kitchen.

One night at the base community, Ann Jaqua, connected the soup kitchen and the Eucharist. She said, "The serving table is like the table in the church, the altar. The two go together. I don't think the Eucharist makes sense without the soup."

I thought of what she'd said a few weeks later when I was

working in the kitchen on Maundy Thursday. I arrived at noon to begin sorting fruit and bread for the lunch to be served. Suddenly, the kitchen felt like worship itself, the altar table in the nearby sanctuary had meaning only because of this table, where I stood, that was full of day-old bread and free grapes.

Karen Torjesen describes "house churches," the meeting places for the early Christians, as "informal, often counter-cultural in tone."[1]

I wondered if the soup kitchen was like one of those early churches, or reminiscent of it, where everyone was welcome or, at least, women, slaves, and artisans were welcome, those people who didn't have authority or even personhood in public life. Maybe in the soup kitchen, we were re-creating the original Eucharist, a feast for the marginal.

> *Maybe in the soup kitchen, we were re-creating the original Eucharist, a feast for the marginal.*

We live in what is thought to be abundance, with lots of stuff to buy. But somehow, it is never enough. In the late eighties, I asked the owner of a successful business, who must have made at least half a million dollars a year, if he had enough money, and he replied, "Don't you understand? There is never enough."

The "never enough" reaches into every aspect of our lives. We don't have enough money, but we also don't have enough time. We don't have enough energy, solitude, or peace. The emotional consequences are subtle and pervasive; we've got fantasy and illusion and anxiety. Believe me, I know them all. So I call the economy we live in "the economy of scarcity."

Here's the irony: the economy of scarcity appears to be abundant, while abundance is marked by an appearance of scarcity. The scarce economy looks rich and full, but within it, people's souls and bodies starve. The economy of abundance, on the other hand, is organized to provide just enough. Like the manna in the desert that could not be stored but was only enough to get through the day, so the economy of abundance releases no more than enough nourishment. I ran out of fruit in the kitchen one day at just the moment a farmer drove up with three cases of oranges.

I don't work in that kitchen anymore, and I miss it. My soul misses it. I am not learning what I learned there about abundant life.

To paraphrase (Episcopal) Bishop Shelby Spong: Did Jesus come to give us religion, to give us the right way to worship? No.

Well then, did Jesus come to teach us how to follow the law, be righteous, be ethical? No.

Did Jesus come to teach us the truth, the one truth against which all other claims can be measured, all heresies decried? To give us orthodoxy?

No. Jesus came to give us life, and life abundant.[2]

Here's the bottom line: if Jesus didn't come to teach us a

system of beliefs, the one true path, or the right way to worship, then what did he come to teach us? Perhaps he came to teach us how to live. Perhaps he came to teach us a way of life that you find out about by living it. It is in the living of that life that we discover what Christianity is, what it means to follow Jesus. The early followers of Jesus didn't have a creed or a codified set of prayers. They did not all worship in the same way. They had some form of baptism and some forms of prayers over bread and wine, and that was about it. They didn't have many of the religious traditions that today we call "Christianity." I suspect they were living by the seat of their pants.

But they had something else. Something that gave them, as is written in Acts, "glad and generous hearts" (Acts 2:46). I got a little whiff of it when I worked in the soup kitchen. I know that many of you have had a taste of it too. It happens when we follow Jesus. It happens when we do what he showed us how to do. The path, as they say, is made by walking it. We participate in the abundant economy when we feed the hungry and visit prisoners. And what if it also breaks through when we live as a community, pool our resources, and redistribute our wealth? Makes you want to throw up, doesn't it?

Jesus knew quite a lot about money. He knew about Caesar and taxes. He knew about the rich young lawyer. He knew about the eye of the needle. He knew about where your treasure is. I don't think Jesus is calling us toward poverty or guilt. I think he calls us toward a glad and generous heart.

I have new respect for those early followers of Jesus because I want it both ways: I want to hoard my money, and at the same time, I long for that abundant life. I want to hide my face from Jesus because I don't want to see his love and compassion. I don't want to see the gulf between my longings and aspirations and the paltriness of my life. I don't want to feel the way you feel when you are on the brink of a high dive. I don't want to know that it doesn't matter how you worship or what you say you believe; it matters how you live.

11

GOING OUT INTO THE WORLD

Something has happened to the bread and the wine.
They have been blessed. What now?

—MARY OLIVER, *THIRST*

THE WORD *PRACTICE* DERIVES FROM THE GREEK WORD *praktikos*, which means "practical" or "concerned with action." All practices are meant, not to be a place where you stay and take a nap, but to lead somewhere, outward toward the world.

As professor and priest Ion Bria has said, there is the "liturgy after the liturgy," that work in the world is inseparable from worship.[1]

> *All practices are meant, not to be a place where you stay and*
> *take a nap, but to lead somewhere, outward toward the world.*

And a friend said that she thinks all of us who are laypersons are people with invisible collars. That is, while ministers and priests are obvious ministers, we are ministers too. It's just that you can't see our collars.

What is being asked of us, those of us with these invisible but demanding collars around our necks? Why should we take Communion or engage in any Christian practice?

In the Gospels, as you can see by now, there are a lot of meal stories, a lot of dinner parties. You would think, given the number of times we hear a parable about eating in the Gospels, that Jesus may have moonlighted as a food critic.

Do you remember the one in which Jesus talks about where you want to be seated? It's in Luke 14:1, 7–14. It's a tricky story, like many of Jesus' parables. The story has two levels, if not several more.

On the first level, he gives us good, practical advice. If you want to avoid being humiliated by taking the wrong seat, go to the one at the bottom of the table. Whatever you do, don't sit at the right hand of the host unless he asks you to. Then, if your host wants to honor you, he will come and get you. We get so wrapped up in thinking of Jesus as a perfect man and a God that we forget he was also simply practical: the truth will make you free; consider the lilies of the field; watch where you sit at a dinner party.

Then, of course, there is the other level to this story. It's about that great dinner party where God is the host. God gets to decide where you are going to sit, who will be exalted. It is not up to us. If we dispense with the idea of God as the Great

Maître d' in the Sky, with a folder of important people and where they will sit, arranged by our own accounting methods (*certainly* she *will be exalted, but not* him), then we can consider this story as about the nature of deep reality.

What was Jesus saying here about what is deeply true? First of all, it may very well be in our DNA, this desire to be next to the important people, in the cherished important seat. We want to be near the big shots who might protect us when the food runs out. Or better yet, we want to be the big shots who will have all the food.

I wonder if Jesus had experience with this situation. We think of him as being perfect from the start and forget he was also human, and he lived as a human being in the world. What I imagine is that for a while at least, he was that bright young rabbi, getting a lot of press, making a splash. He probably sat at the right hand of the leader of the Pharisees fairly often. Enough to get used to it.

And then, a few years or a few weeks or a few days later, when he wasn't quite what the leadership wanted, he may have found himself sitting way, way down at the foot. I know that Jesus is in many ways different from me, more mysterious and certainly much more faithful and loving and brave, but I also want to think that he is like me, that he understands some of my struggle because he struggled with the same demons. I think he may very well have wanted to be famous and exalted and discovered the hard way where that leads.

A recent book calls it "status anxiety."[2] It's not easy, working this one out. It isn't easy when we are all awash in it. How big is your house? How new is your car? How about your clothes? Your jewelry? Or let's get more subtle: do you drop the mention of recent travel into your conversation? Or the names of important people?

We can talk about status anxiety in church and our need to be exalted and come up with wise things to say about it, but tomorrow, at work or at a dinner party, it will come up again. I know it will for me. And part of what I want to know is, not only how do I keep myself humble, but what is humility anyway? And how do I deal with those who exalt themselves? And by the way, when will the first be last?

> *Part of what I want to know is, not only how do I keep myself humble, but what is humility anyway?*

For example, there's a woman in the apartment building in New York where we often stay who dresses in head-to-toe Prada, leaves her dog alone when she goes on vacation so it barks all night, and talks on her cell phone in the elevator. I want to know, when is she going to get her comeuppance? And those incredibly cold and contemptuous people I saw in a famously rich oceanside cove—what about them? We are surrounded by people focused on exalting the self. Everywhere. And it has probably always been like this. Always, human beings have strived for power over others, have sought to be exalted, have gathered up wealth. And in the United States, because we believe that the playing field is level, many of us think we deserve to be exalted. And whatever exaltation we have, we want more. We think we deserve more. We rarely think we deserve less. I mean, what if what we have is not what we actually deserve if God were really, really fair, but more than we deserve, given to us by grace?

Exalted is from Middle English: *ex*—out, and *altus*, high—as in "altar, high up." It is like that lovely name for a group of birds: an exaltation of larks. *Humble* is from Middle English and Latin and Old French: *humilis* means low, lowly, from *humus*, ground.

So if you are exalted, you are lifted high up, even as high as the altar. And if you are humbled, you are in the *humus*, in touch with the ground.

And there is one little problem with being exalted: it relies on what others think of you. Someone has to do the exalting. Someone has to lift you up. A president, a bishop, a book award committee, a reviewer, your boss, your family, the local chamber of commerce, a food critic, you fill in the blanks. And exaltation depends on being lifted up *over* other people. I sat in first class during two legs of my book tour one year—I think it was a gift to my publisher from the airline—and, yes, immediately, I felt myself not only deserving of first class but also condescending toward those people who slogged past me on their way to the back of the plane.

There is one little problem with being exalted:
it relies on what others think of you.

It's perfectly fine to be recognized and honored for your work or your children's good upbringing or your fantastic chocolate cake. For your art or your writing or your singing or your dancing or your acting or your accounting or your good arguing in court. We all need and deserve recognition from our fellow human beings, and I say the more the merrier. But being honored is different from exalting yourself. Different from not only sitting in first class but being condescending to those who aren't. Different from not only winning the prize, but looking down on those who didn't. Different from not only sitting at the right hand of your famous host, but separating yourself from those at the foot of the table. I once heard a woman complain to the mayor of my town that the homeless people in her neighborhood were spoiling her view.

At one point on that same airplane, a woman got on who was injured, walking with crutches, and it occurred to me that as this seat had been given to me, I could give it to her. It would have been much more comfortable for her to sit in the front of the plane. Did I do this? I did not. And thus I think I missed out on something that day.

Many of us have read C. S. Lewis's *The Great Divorce*, his allegorical novel about heaven and hell. One of the novel's most memorable scenes is the one in which the narrator is being given a sort of tour of heaven. He sees a beautiful lady walking toward him and assumes by her beauty and her attendants that she is Mary, the Queen of Heaven, but no, his angel guide tells him: she is Sarah Smith, who lived at Golders Green, a suburban enclave of London, which was largely populated when the novel was written (this is the best part of the story) by Jews. It turns out that Sarah Smith was a nobody while living on the earth. But she is exalted in heaven, the angel tells the narrator, because "every boy who met her became her son and every girl her daughter and every beast and bird that came near her had its place in her love. In her, they became themselves."[3] Sarah Smith knew something about the nature of deep reality, the truth about life, the bottom line, the thing for which I know we will be exalted, which is how much we love. How much we free ourselves from everything that keeps us from loving and being loved: how much we free ourselves from competition, constraint, self-pity, and self-importance. All the things that stand between us and love.

A friend of mine invited me out to lunch several years ago and told me a fairly horrendous story about his family: his high school–age daughter had gotten pregnant and insisted on having the baby. She had, in fact, just had the little boy a few days before he and I had lunch. My friend and his wife had tried very hard in the early days of her pregnancy to get her to give up the child for adoption, but the girl refused. I sat there listening to the story, and all kinds of words of advice rose in my head. I can't remember anymore what they were; they were so completely beside the point.

When he had finished telling the story, I was about to wade in, when he picked up his wallet and pulled out a picture of an incredibly cute baby boy. "Here he is," he said, and a huge smile spread all over his face. "We've never had a boy in the family before." I looked at the photo and I looked at his face. What came to me then felt as close to grace as I have ever felt. We were sitting in a museum cafe, and I felt as if the room were slowed down to God speed. All of the words of advice evaporated from my mind. I don't remember exactly what I said, but what I realized was it's all about love. It's all about increasing our capacity to love. It was as clear as a bell. Whatever happened, my friend loved that baby, and it looked to me as though, if he kept loving that baby, his life would be better, and so would be that baby's life, and the baby's mother's life, and so forth and so on, and the rest was just commentary.

(Lest any of us make this story into a formula, it's not one. It doesn't mean that high school girls should have babies. I am not sure anything in life works by formula.)

To be exalted by earthly standards is to be constantly aware of who is not exalted or to be looking over one's shoulder for who might be more exalted next. It is to be anxious. To be exalted by heavenly standards is to urge others to be exalted, too, to share in the bounty of being loved and loving.

To be exalted by heavenly standards is to urge others to be exalted, too, to share in the bounty of being loved and loving.

At our base community meeting, we had a new person join us. I'll call him Frank. Frank dropped in and introduced himself as a newcomer to Trinity and a newly arrived person to Santa Barbara. He was here, he said, because he needed good medical care. I thought Frank was probably somewhere in his fifties. He turned out to be in his seventies. He was chubby, friendly, well spoken, and very well educated. Over the weeks, he quoted Tillich and Kant. He was lighthearted; when he smiled, his face really did light up. He was not perfect. Sometimes he talked too much. But he was truly appreciative of what others said; it gave him pleasure, I think, to appreciate. He said once that you could lose everything, but the self still survived, and although this could readily be a cliché on another's lips, I believed it coming from Frank.

One day, Ann Jaqua happened to be talking about the Community Kitchen, the soup kitchen that she started and we both worked in. Frank fairly beamed at her. He said, "You started the Community Kitchen? Why, that's great. It serves the best food of any place I've been."

I think we all sort of gaped at him for a few seconds. I realized in those long seconds that Frank was homeless because he was eating at the soup kitchen. It turned out he was living at the local homeless shelter. And I had not known it. He was sitting at the table with the rest of us, nice, middle-class, employed, housed, and he was sitting at that table with absolute equal standing, no more and no less. It made me proud of the church. It also made me think about what we learn by having someone like Frank in our midst. Or I will say, what I learned. I learned that health care for the poor in Santa Barbara is better than in LA. That housing for the poor is good in LA and also good in Washington, D.C. And that you can lose everything, but the self still survives. And I saw in Frank humility, a matter-of-fact humility; he had his feet on the ground, he was grounded in something that could last for a long time, maybe forever.

And of course I think of him at the table in the library as I write about all of us at the table at Communion. I think of how, at the great table in the sky, none of us will know, finally, where we will be sitting, and we will not know who will be sitting next to us. And we will not know who is more important and who is less important. It will all be a big surprise. I imagine that Frank will take the lowliest seat he can find, knowing his place, and that someone, probably Jesus, will go up to him and whisper in his ear that he should get up and follow him to a better place at the table.

But actually, when I really imagine it, I realize that where we sit will be based on where we want to sit. If we want to sit at a table with a lot of people bickering about who is more exalted, that's where we'll end up. And if we want to sit at a table where everyone is full of joy and love and discovery, we'll sit there. And, of course, we don't actually have to wait until we get to that final table. We could choose right now.

Jesus lived here with us, broke bread with us, lived the life of a human in the world. He was executed by powers that would not let him live, that saw in him a threat so great they had to torture and then kill him. Three days after his death, his disciples experienced him as living: he walked among them, he broke bread once again, he cooked fish on a beach, and he reminded them, above all else, to forgive.

Most of us, I think, imagine heaven as a far-off place in the sky. It's an image from childhood, like God as an old man with a white beard sitting on a throne amid the clouds. Because of this image, we imagine that those who die, die out, as Miriam MacGillis, a Dominican sister, said. We die out—*Whoom!*—go up to heaven. But there is another way to think of dying and where we go. Instead, we die in, MacGillis continues; that is, we reenter earth, to be part of the earth that gave us our beginning, to become part of all that lives, and moves, and has its being (Acts 17:28). What if the risen Christ does not die out, as in being lifted into the heavens, but rather dies in, that is, dies into the whole of the world?

> *What if the risen Christ does not die out, as in being lifted into the heavens, but rather dies in, that is, dies into the whole of the world?*

My brother, Kit, died in 1996, of cancer, at the age of fifty-two. He was my only brother, my only sibling. Cancer deaths, as many of you probably know, are most often hard deaths. He died slowly, week by week. And week by week, I sat at his side.

My brother worked as a surveyor. He walked all over New Mexico mapping the Rio Grande basin for the Bureau of Land Management. He told me that in order to survey, you always have to have two points. I have a picture of him, leaning over his tripod and looking through the scope, high above a bridge in northern New Mexico. He's looking for a distant point on the other side of the river. I thought of him then and I think of him now as making sense of geography.

One afternoon when my brother was dying, he was lying on the couch in his living room, in the room he built himself in Polvadera, New Mexico, out of adobe bricks and pine beams. It was spring, as it is now, and in New Mexico in the spring, the wind blows all the time, stirring up the dust. Kit and I were looking out at the yard, at the apricot tree he planted when he was first doing chemo, at the plum blossoms and the cotton-wood trees and beyond that, the sky. All of a sudden, he said, "Look!" I tried to see what he was seeing, but all I saw was the window and the trees and the sky. He saw something else. I was sure then and I am sure now, that he saw another point, this one farther away than any he had sighted before.

He died at three o'clock in the morning. After we had

signed all the papers, said good-bye to the hospice nurse, and finally, said good-bye to Kit, and they took him away in the undertaker's hearse, my husband and I went back to our hotel to get some sleep. I remember that I felt then as if everything in my life was in pieces, like an archeological dig before the archeologists get there, shards on the ground. Nothing made any sense. The power of death is awesome; its mass destruction shredded my life.

The disciples must have felt this way. I am sure. Everything they had was destroyed in one afternoon.

But that is not the end of their story, and it is not the end of mine. Later that day, after I woke up, I paced the hall of the hotel, talked to my family on the phone, worked on the hard business of death: the papers, the cremation, the obituary. Then I got in the rental car, alone, and drove out to a bird refuge my brother loved. Earlier in the year, when he was still able to walk, he and I, and his wife and my husband, had gone out there. It's a huge refuge, the Bosque de Apache, with birds from all over the world. When we all visited together, it was evening, and the sandhill cranes were coming in to feed and rest for the night. They are big birds, and the way they land is truly awesome. They drop down out of the sky, close to the water, and then they suddenly put out their wings, to brake themselves, huge wings and long legs stretched beneath them. They almost stop in the air. And then they land, sometimes in inches of water. When I saw the first batch land that evening, I squealed in delight, and my brother said something about not being able to take me to any nice places anymore.

But now he was gone. When I got out there, the light was turning to evening. I walked out onto the paths along the dikes between the ponds. None of the fancy birds were left: the sand-hill cranes were gone, as well as the snow geese. But there were red-winged blackbirds, Canada geese, and ducks, making their soft sounds. The light was falling evenly on the bulrushes, the yellow millet, and the water. A huge black bird was dive-bombing each pond, and the little birds rose and flocked before him and then settled back.

I was looking out at the bulrushes when I saw something else. I saw, or understood, that Kit was there. His singular, unique life. He was there somehow, burning in the bulrushes, in the light and in the birds. It was as if his life were exploding into them, and was about to become them, and I had been given the miraculous luck to catch him just as he dove in. He was traveling at a great speed, it seemed to me, into the place where all things are alive. I reached toward him, hardly able to believe it, wanting to hold on to him and to the moment, sheltering my hope in doubt. I thought, *He is alive.*

We know from the work of physicists that the very material from which life arose was dust blown here from some distant star that we will never see. That the world is made of shapes and material that move and change, things we cannot know, exactly, but often can only apprehend. That carbon dioxide atoms that surround you today may have been breathed out by a woman or a man who lived where you live hundreds of years ago. We can say that the distant point my brother saw as he lay dying, may exist, not visible to us as we go about the business of living, but later, as we come near another threshold. And that my experience of Kit's life entering into the life of the world, strange and hard to describe as it is, may be similar to what the writers of the resurrection stories in the gospels were trying to convey.

The life of Jesus, if it is meaningful to us, is meant to reveal the nature of God. Jesus' life is like a lens or an icon through which we might glimpse the truth about God's nature, and the nature of the world.

> *The life of Jesus, if it is meaningful to us,*
> *is meant to reveal the nature of God.*

After the resurrection, Jesus the Resurrected One, now the Christ, is everywhere.

Luther put it beautifully in one of his Table Talks. He tells the story of how his wife, Katie (Katherina von Bora) complained that he was always talking about Christ's presence as being something in the here and now, but she could not see him. "Where is this Lord Christ of whom you constantly speak?" she asked. Luther responded that Christ is everywhere, "in the beans in your bean garden, Katie; in the rocks out there, and even in the rope around some poor hopeless man's neck."

Christ is everywhere. In the beans in your bean garden, in the waters of the lakes and rivers and mountains held sacred by the first American nations, in the rocks and the trees, and, yes, even in the fabric of the hoods that were placed over the heads of the prisoners in Abu Gharib prison in Iraq. Yes, even in that place, where both captive and guard are imprisoned. No hell is powerful enough to keep out resurrection life. Nothing can separate us from the love of God. Christ is everywhere, his life not parceled out in scarcity, only there on a throne in heaven or only here among the good churchgoing people, but abundantly present everywhere, freely given, everywhere where things long to be whole and loving and struggle to be free.

Christ is everywhere, especially in bread and wine, where, as Luther says, he binds himself and us to each other. By this we are to understand that God is meant to be breathed in, God is meant to be bathed in, and finally, God is meant to be eaten. God is part of the daily, heartbreaking reality of our lives, in the air, in the floors, in the sweat, in the blood, and in the tears.

> *Christ is everywhere, especially in bread and wine, where,*
> *as Luther says, he binds himself and us to each other.*

It's Easter Sunday. A group of men are in prison. They are part of the more than ten thousand political prisoners in this country's jails. They want to celebrate Communion, but they have no wine, no bread, no cup, no priest. The non-Christian prisoners say to them, "We will help you. We will talk quietly so you can meet together and not draw the attention of the prison guards."

"We have no bread, not even water to use as wine," their leader says to them, "but we will act as though we have."

And so he begins to lead them in the Communion service from the Episcopal Book of Common Prayer that he has memorized over many years of attending church. When he gets to the words of Jesus said during the Eucharist prayer, he turns to the man standing next to him, holds out his empty hands, and says, "This is my body, which is given for you."

And so as they go around the circle, one by one, each man turns to the next man, opens his palms, and says, "This is my body, given for you."

If Christ is everywhere, he is in us. We are his body now, his hands and his feet. We are all the ongoing incarnation.

Go out into the world, knowing you are blessed.

NOTES

Chapter 2: Communion Is a Practice
1. Heda Kovaly, *Under a Cruel Star: A Life in Prague, 1941–1968* (Teaneck, NJ: Holmes and Meier, 1997), 52.
2. Walter Brueggemann, *The Prophetic Imagination* (Minneapolis: Fortress Press, 1978), 85.
3. Ibid.
4. *Moonstruck*, written by Robert Patrick Shanley, 1987.

Chapter 3: Waiting
1. Josephus, *Jewish Antiquities* 1:194–95

Chapter 4: Receiving
1. Jill Bolte Taylor, "My Stroke of Insight," TED.com, March 2008.
2. Ibid.

Chapter 5: Afterward
1. Simone Weil, *Waiting for God* (New York: Harper and Row, 1951), 63.
2. Taylor, "My Stroke of Insight."
3. Elizabeth Gilbert, *Eat, Pray, Love* (New York: Penguin Press, 2007), "Pray" section.

Chapter 6: Eating the Body and Blood
1. Kathryn Harrison, *While They Slept: An Inquiry into the Murder of a Family*, as quoted in a review by Robert Pinsky, *New York Times* Sunday Book Review, June 8, 2008.

Chapter 7: Magic and Thanksgiving

1. Stephen F. de Borhegyi, *El Sanctuario de Chimayo* (Santa Fe: The Spanish Colonial Arts Society, Inc., 1956) 6.
2. Eric Eckholm, "A Pastor Begs to Differ with Flock on Miracles," *New York Times*, February 20, 2008.
3. Ibid.
4. David Ehrenfeld, *Beginning Again* (New York: Oxford Press, 1993) 9.

Chapter 8: Myths and Traditions

1. Flannery O'Connor, *Habit of Being* (New York: Farrar, Straus and Giroux, 1988), 125.
2. C. S. Lewis, *An Experiment in Criticism* (Cambridge: Cambridge University Press, 1961) 138.
3. Simone Weil, *Waiting for God* (New York: Putnam, 1951), 102.
4. Flannery O'Connor, *The Violent Bear It Away* (New York: Macmillan, 2007), 241.

Chapter 9: A History in Brief

1. Helen B. Volz, "A New Taste of Communion" (transcript from UUFCC Service, February 5, 2006), 4, http://www.uufcc.com/Lay/UUFCC Service February 5 Communion Volz.pdf.
2. Paul Bradshaw, ed., *The New Westminster Dictionary of Liturgy and Worship* (Louisville: John Knox Press, 2003).
3. Paul Bradshaw, quoting Justin Martyr in *Eucharistic Origins* (Oxford: Oxford University Press, 2004), 62.
4. Paul Bradshaw, *The Search for the Origins of Christian Worship* (Oxford: Oxford University Press, 1992) 124.
5. Bradshaw, *The New Westminster Dictionary of Liturgy and Worship*, 136.
6. Ibid., 135.
7. *The Book of Common Prayer* (Oxford: Oxford University Press, 1897), 563.
8. Phyllis Tickle, *The Great Emergence* (Grand Rapids, MI: Baker, 2008).

9. Kenan B. Osborne in Paul Bradshaw, ed., *The New Westminster Dictionary of Liturgy and Worship* (Louisville: John Knox Press, 2003), 204.

Chapter 10: The Soup Kitchen

1. Karen Torjesen, *When Women Were Priests* (San Francisco: Harper/San Francisco, 1991), 6, 11.
2. John Shelby Spong, *The Bishop's Voice: Selected Essays* 1979–1999, (New York: The Crossroad Publishing Company, 1999) 233.

Chapter 11: Going Out into the World

1. Ion Bria, *The Liturgy After the Liturgy* (Geneva: World Council of Churches, 1996).
2. Alain de Botton, *Status Anxiety* (New York: Pantheon Books, 2004).
3. C. S. Lewis, *The Great Divorce* (New York: Macmillan, 1946), 107.

ABOUT THE AUTHOR

Nora Gallagher is a native of New Mexico, where she was educated at St. John's College.

She is the author of *Things Seen and Unseen: A Year Lived in Faith* and *Practicing Resurrection: A Memoir of Work, Doubt, Discernment, and Moments of Grace*, as well as the novel *Changing Light*, which is being adapted for film.

She was a fellow at both the MacDowell Colony and Blue Mountain Center.

She is preacher-in-residence at Trinity Episcopal Church, Santa Barbara, and sits on the advisory board of the Yale Divinity School. She lives with her husband, novelist and poet Vincent Stanley, in Santa Barbara and New York.

THE ANCIENT PRACTICES SERIES

PHYLLIS TICKLE, GENERAL EDITOR

Finding Our Way Again by Brian McLaren

In Constant Prayer by Robert Benson

Sabbath by Dan B. Allender

Fasting by Scot McKnight

The Sacred Meal by Nora Gallagher

The Liturgical Year by Joan Chittister

Stand at the crossroads and look; ask for the ancient paths,
ask where the good way is, and walk in it,
and you will find rest for your souls.

—JEREMIAH 6:16 NIV

THOMAS NELSON
Since 1798